YORKSHIRE RELISH

Also by Elizabeth Cragoe

BUTTERCUPS AND DAISY
COWSLIPS AND CLOVER

YORKSHIRE RELISH

ELIZABETH CRAGOE

HAMISH HAMILTON
LONDON

To Thomas and Elspeth,
as a thank-you

First published in Great Britain 1978
by Hamish Hamilton Ltd
90 Great Russell Street London WC1B 3PT

Copyright © 1978 by Elizabeth Cragoe

British Library Cataloguing in Publication Data

Cragoe, Elizabeth
    Yorkshire relish.
    1. West Yorkshire, Eng. – Social life and customs
    2. Country life – England – West Yorkshire
    I. Title
    942.8'1'0830924   DA70.W498
    ISBN 0-241-20054-2

Printed in Great Britain by
Western Printing Services Ltd, Bristol

CONTENTS

ONE

THE NURSERY

It was a goldfish that opened my eyes to the way of the world—a goldfish called Percy. I was three at the time and dead innocent. If you'd told me that Santa Claus was the King of England I'd have believed you. I believed anything.

Not that Percy *told* me anything exactly; for if I was dead innocent, he was just dead and that is no help in telling. He died from a surfeit of confetti that Richard and I gave him in mistake for ant-eggs, and his death being clearly our fault gave us a good deal of remorse. But if Percy hadn't died, I would not have had two goldfish bowls to play with in the bath and my first experience of the sucker-punch might have been delayed a little longer.

There was no room for the bowls in the bath when we were all in it. For with three of us all in together, it was a tight fit. Gillian sat at the narrow end, which was the best place, but that was fair enough. She was six. And Richard was five, so he sat down by the taps. And I was the youngest and the smallest, so I sat sideways in the middle, legs bent up like a frog's and soap-rack rubbing my shoulder, and as long as they both played fair with their feet it worked, after a fashion.

But Gillian was out now. It was Monday, which was toenail cutting night, and Nurse's head, haloed in golden steam, had popped round the door to summon her into the nursery. And she had gone, swathed in a towel. I ducked thankfully under the soap-rack and surfaced at the other side. There was room and to spare now, and carefully taking the two glass globes off the corner of the bath I half-filled them with murky water and set them to float. One was a little one in which Percy had arrived from the fair where he'd been won; the other, much bigger, he'd been put into later.

Richard was struggling to pass his big toe through a small hole in the face flannel and murmuring a story to himself as he did so. 'And the Captain *would* do it. And his mother told him not to and his nurse told him not to and they said "If you put it through a little hole like that it'll go black and gangrenous and drop off." But the Captain *would* do it . . . and in the end it *did* go black and gangrenous . . .' He withdrew his toe with an effort and some water splashed over the edge, 'and it *did* drop off. I bet I could drink a whole goldfish bowl of this water.'

'What, bathwater?' I asked, shocked. Richard regarded me calculatingly. 'Well, of course' he said. 'Didn't you know? People drink it all the time. But you couldn't drink much, of course, because you're only little. But I can. Gillian and I often drink bathwater, much dirtier than this—heaps and heaps of it. I could drink that big goldfish bowl full of bathwater before you could even drink half of the little one. I bet you!'

That was enough. If that was what the big ones did, I must do it too, and without more ado I filled the small bowl raised it to my lips and began to drink.

It did taste funny—as well it might; for three children who have played out all day in a heavy woollen manufacturing area pick up a good deal of soot, and the water was black with it now. A good deal of Lux had been used to remove the soot from our bodies and I could taste that too, high, sweet and scented. But if the big ones did it . . . I quaffed away, stopping for a pant now and again, but doggedly resuming my task and amazed at the way the level in Richard's bowl kept dropping, as he had boasted it would, much faster than mine.

And then came disillusionment. For Richard, no longer able to restrain his giggles at the success of his confidence trick, joggled the bowl against his teeth—and all at once I saw that whereas I had been really drinking, he had been pouring his discreetly down his chin and down over his already wet chest back into the bath! Oh! the death of innocence! But it comes to us all, and many, I suppose, have paid for it in a much harder currency than a quart of dirty bathwater.

The door opened and Nurse came briskly in. 'Come on you two!' she said. 'Jump out now. Wrap up in your towels and run into the nursery, there's a lovely fire. Richard, what's all this water on the floor?'

2

The only untoward result of my copious draughts of dirty bathwater was that I had to get up an hour or so later to go to the lavatory, and that was frightening. If Nurse had been there it would have been all right, but she had gone downstairs. You could hear her moving about in the nursery for a bit after she had put the light out, clearing things away and getting our clothes ready for the next day, and usually we were asleep before she went down; but my bladder knew it could never hold a quart all night and nagged me awake every time my head touched the pillow. I didn't at all want to listen to it, to leave the safety of the warm double bed I shared with Gillian and venture into the no man's land of the landing, but it was that or wet the bed, so eventually I had to go.

The landing light was on, that was one comfort. It had an orange shade which cast a lovely glow on the thick brown carpet, but the worst bit was to come. For in the lavatory lived a terrible monster, and to dare him alone, at eight o'clock at night was probably the bravest thing I had ever done in my life. Leaving the door wide open, I crept into the lavatory. It was a matter of the nicest timing. The creature, who lived in the cistern, was called the Clockneinst, and although none of us had ever seen him Richard said he was there. When you pulled the chain he gave a kind of sighing gulp before the water rushed into the lavatory and that was his moment of power. If you weren't lucky—and who could say how long one's luck might last?—it was at that moment that he would come out and 'get' you. But if you were poised just right, with the door open, and if you set off running as fast as you could, even as you pulled, you might get back to the bedroom before he could jump down from the tank. And once the full rush of water came down, he was defused, so to speak, for that time, and had to climb back again, thwarted and grumbling, and all the keener to catch you on another occasion. In fear and trembling I pulled the chain and shot off down the landing. And lo and behold, I had done it! I was still all right. Thankfully I burrowed down in the warmth again and turned on my side to sleep. And the street lamp in the road threw huge shadows on the curtains through the leaves of the Turkey oak, and the millgirls on their way back from the first house of the pictures screamed with raucous laughter, and

3

their high heels went click-click-click-click-click all the way up the pavement. . .

Ours was a large, square, peaceful sort of house, built of stone and standing in an acre and a half of garden. It was set in the village of Knearsley, a manufacturing community of about ten thousand souls which lay halfway between the two great wool cities of Leeds and Bradford; my father was the village doctor. My mother was a doctor too, but when we were young children she did not work. She began to practise medicine again when the war broke out and my father's partner was called up; and somehow, miraculously, in spite of doing a job that started at 9 in the morning and rarely finished before 8 at night—not to mention night alarms—she still managed to run the house so that it remained what it had always been—warm, glowing, generous—a home to be loved.

You took the midday sunshine straight on your brow when you came out of our front door and stood on the big stone steps that led down to the garden. In front of you stretched the lawns, broad and peaceful, striped from the mowing machine and dappled with shadows from the narrow belts of trees that screened them from view down both their long sides. A twelve-foot beech hedge along the bottom made a background for the blue spires of the delphiniums that flickered like brandy flames above the wealth of a double herbaceous border. Lupins stood like standards of gold and rose, purple and crimson, and fragrant trusses of pinks tumbled over the stones at the border edge. Velvet pansies lifted their innocent-looking cat-faces among the taller things, and showers of roses in every colour from bronze and yellow to tenderest pink and deepest madder dripped their lavish profusion of petals to carpet the ground round their feet.

There was a sharp change of level halfway along the lawn which we always called the Little Hill. It was daisy-studded, and good for rolling down. Two big old Siberian crab-apple trees leaned over its edges, and in April the pink lace of their blossom showered down on the daffodils that grew there so thickly that their crisp frilly petticoats squeaked and rustled as they jostled against one another.

Our house had been built in about 1860 when an era of great prosperity for the woollen industry had led to a great boom in mill-building and an equivalent rash of new houses. The tiny villages where the hand-workers had lived, spinning, weaving, or finishing, as the case might be, were lost in the high tide of industrialism and swelled abruptly to many times their original size. Or perhaps it is wrong to say they were lost. They still kept their identity even if they were now mere beads on the string that joined Leeds to Bradford, and the new developments were organic, unlike some of the characterless dormitory suburbs of today. For the vast majority of the village's inhabitants still worked in the village, and the Victorian builders had catered for the whole spectrum of human prosperity. There were poor houses for the lowest-paid hands, and decent terraces for the more skilled. There were stone-built villas, semi-detached, for the managerial classes and larger houses like ours for doctors, lawyers, parsons, and the owners of small mills. Top of the market was for the big mill-owners who were really pretty rich. They lived in great houses with libraries and billiard-rooms, set in the middle of well-timbered twenty-acre parks and surrounded by high stone walls; their doors were opened by parlour-maids in frilly caps with long streamers, and they drove back from their labours at the mill in the plushy silence of chauffeur-driven Rolls Royces.

There was one mark of respectability that came with the house which divided the sheep from the goats with the unerring precision of a Nancy Mitford, and that was the trees on the lawn. For trees there had to be, and not trees that you could plant yourself. They had to be there, full grown, and they had to be the right kind. The two acceptable species that had been planted at the time of building in front of every house of any pretensions were the wych elm and the weeping ash, and luckily we had them both. There they stood, four-square and spacious, set wide apart on the top lawn and their clean undistorted growth seemed to emphasise the virtue and solidity that were the house's main characteristics.

It was a well-built house. The only photograph we have of it shows it mantled in ivy, as it was in our early years, but later we stripped that off and saw for the first time the superb quality of the masonry. The front of the house was particularly fine. It was built of the local sandstone squared into blocks about two

5

foot by one foot and jointed with the utmost precision. There was less than a quarter of an inch of mortar between these great slabs of stone, and the dressing was even more remarkable. For they were smoothed to their shape in a series of tiny ridges, chipped by hand with a mason's chisel and running parallel with the short side of the block. And when you looked closely you could see that the long-dead workmen who wrought those blocks had chiselled the dressing-lines a bare eighth of an inch apart all over the stone, and had not strayed the least bit from the true vertical line even in the largest blocks. It was lovely work.

Inside, the house continued in the same style of solidity with an unobtrusive excellence that we can now no longer take for granted. Doors were big and solid, and shut with a sonorous 'clonk'. Door-frames kept their squareness and were properly keyed into the walls. Large sash windows slid up and down in their grooves at the touch of a finger, and the tall wooden shutters that folded back into the wall fitted closely enough to make an adequate black-out, when the time came for it to be needed.

Other big houses like ours, with generous gardens, followed the leafy curve of the road away to the south until it joined the main road, and a park with playing fields and recreation grounds formed the view through the trees away to the left. But it was not completely idyllic. You could never forget for long that you were in a manufacturing area, for the towering mill-stacks trailed their sooty plumes on every horizon; and the voice of the thrush in the dewy elm tree could not entirely block out the distant roar of traffic and the banshee wails of the mill buzzers in the morning.

The same contrasts marked the lives of the people who lived in the various houses that made up our village. I was born in 1930, the youngest of three, and I know with hindsight that even by 1933, the year I first remember, times for the working poor were pretty hard. The slump of 1929 had not really passed away and there was a good deal of unemployment. And in those days unemployment meant near-starvation, and a total lack of many amenities that we have now come to take for granted. It was not rare, for instance, to see little boys barefooted, and wearing rags

6

that showed great areas of their skinny, pale grey, under-nourished torsos through the rents. Ours was a largely working class practice and my parents saw plenty of distress and did what they could to alleviate it. And one of the ways in which this could best be done was by the provision of jobs, so everyone who was comfortably off employed as many people as they could afford to support, and the money circulated to everyone's benefit.

But of course questions of economics and social justice had no meaning for us children and the world as it touched our lives was good. When the sun shone, we played in our leafy, lawny garden, and when the rain fell we amused ourselves just as happily indoors.

Our nursery was a pleasant room. On the first floor, its big window looked south over the garden, and a bright fire burned in the fireplace behind a tall mesh fireguard with a brass top rail. A square of Turkey carpet, glowing red, covered most of the floor, and an old walnut upright piano stood against the wall. There was a rocking horse by the window, a classic dapple grey galloper with staring glass eyes and a flowing tail, and a doll's house, small and dilapidated, in the corner. The table was a round one of oak on a pedestal leg, country-made, in the simple style of the eighteenth century, and on it we drew, wrote, modelled, painted, and had tea. A clean white cloth was laid on it for this ceremony and milk, bread-and-butter and home-made raspberry jam were brought up from the kitchen; but otherwise it stood usefully bare.

There were chairs in the nursery too—solid, Victorian ones that have come to be worth a lot of money; and there was a big press, with cupboards for toys and drawers for our clothes. But there was still a lot of room for play.

The arbiter of our play was Nurse and we were lucky in that she was young, amiable and diplomatic, avoiding by deft manage-ment awkward scenes, clashes of will, or exhibitions of tempera-ment; and as a bonus to add to all these other good qualities, she was also beautiful. She had short, curly golden hair ('Why is your hair all dark round the parting, Nurse?') deep blue eyes, and a neat figure, not too straight up and down. She wore a white overall that was always fresh and starched. She was kind and even-tempered; she listened to our chat, took us for walks, doled out malt and cod liver oil or milk of magnesia as need occasioned, and was not too particular about toys being left lying on the nursery floor.

There were a lot of toys. There was Quacky, a duck, Sandy, Bobby, and Brownstair, who were dogs, and a tall handsome Golliwog called Hansel. There was Gretel, a baby doll with shutting eyes, and a tiny celluloid doll whose sole purpose was to be put between the last two and be christened 'And' which we thought very witty. There was Red Riding Hood with her cloak and her long brown hair, and Burrows, an elegant rabbit; but pride and darling of all and everybody's best beloved, there was Redspot.

Redspot was a dog in a sitting-up position and what was the secret of his charisma I can now no longer remember, but he certainly had more than his share. He was white pretty well all over, for his ears had faded, and his eyes had gone, and the one spot of colour about his threadbare person was the little scarlet tongue that had given him his name. He spoke often, through any one of us, in a special accent, revealing a character that was both cynical and opportunist, but like a traditional white clown in a circus he could do no wrong.

We often took him to school with us in the little dame school we all attended and it was here that a terrible catastrophe befell him from which he was only saved by the ingenuity of Nurse. For we showed him to Miss Allen, our schoolmistress, one day in the fondness of our zeal and she took him into her hands the better to admire him. And then, with a most uncharacteristic failure of understanding, she said brightly 'Poor Redspot's lost his eyes! Let's make him some new ones—look.' And while we stood horror-struck before her she seized a pen and inked in two great, hostile staring orbs on the kindly white countenance of our beloved! Richard and Gillian stared, aghast, but I burst out crying and seized Redspot, rushed out of the room, and bellowed all the way home. Luckily it was lunchtime.

I could not eat my lunch. Redspot came into the dining room with us and every time I raised my eyes from my plate I saw afresh those dreadful daubs that mocked his face with a hideous expression not his own. Sobs choked me and as

8

soon as I was allowed to leave the table I hurried up to the nursery and crouched up in a corner behind the curtain for a good mope.

But before I had been there five minutes there was a sound of flying feet on the stairs and the door burst open. Richard and Gillian came tumbling in. In their hands they bore Redspot. 'Look, look!' they cried. 'Nurse has done it. He's all right again, look!' and, unbelieving, I looked; and with the relief of one who awakens from a nightmare I saw again the dear blank face, those hateful eyes gone and the only colour the little red spot of that cheeky protruding tongue! How was it done? I did not enquire, it was enough that he was restored; but tennis shoe whitener was the means of our deliverance.

None of the other toys was quite in the Redspot league for popularity. There was a decided social structure. Redspot was king, and then came the vast bulk of the toys which we liked but did not love. And then there were the others. Some of them were toys which had developed sharp personalities, like the nesting set of Russian wooden dolls which had acquired the peevish protesting voice of a witch-like old woman who lived up the road. 'Eh! What are you doing, Eh?' she would creak, sharply, as you unscrewed her, until finally (with a change of spelling) it became not only her name but a generic term for all her kind which are called 'Ay-what-are-you-doing-ays' to this day. Other toys were vapid and only slightly unpleasant, like Rita Botty-ache who had a pointed head and met all ill usage with a resigned Christian smile.

But the worst doll of all was Violet who was obviously created just to be an enemy. She was a cloth doll stuffed with sawdust and the look on her face was a compound of vacancy, pride, self-satisfaction and smugness in equal proportions. She had short spiky fair hair and round, staring blue eyes, and like Redspot, she did a lot of talking. But where Redspot was daring, urbane and delightful, Violet was just awful. She had a high-pitched, whining, sing-song voice and her whole conversation consisted of self-praise adorned with characteristic exclamations which only served to emphasise the essential vileness of her personality. She had only one theme: 'Ee-jow-ee-jow-ee-jow-ee-jow!' she would exclaim, smirking admiringly at her reflection in the

9

mirror. 'I-yam-a-very-good-girl! I-yam-so-pretty! I-yam-such-a-very-nice-girl! Ee-jow-ee-jow-ee-jow-ee-jow!' It was too much. Nobody could like her.

In the end we crucified her. It was Miss Allen who all un-wittingly gave us the idea in a scripture lesson just before Easter when she told us all the terrible things that had been done to Our Saviour with a wealth of technical detail that completely captured our imaginations. We went home wild to crucify some-thing; it was a form of punishment we had never even heard of before and it seemed particularly suited to one so hardened in villainy as Violet. So we took her down to the sandpit and nailed her to a cross made of purloined firewood and she hung there very realistically giving us intense artistic satisfaction.

After the proper number of hours had elapsed we un-nailed her and put Ponds cold cream into the holes in her hands and feet as the best available substitute for myrrh and then we put her in the bottom drawer of the dressing-table in our bedroom where she remained for the statutory three days. On the third day she rose again but unlike her great Original she ascended not into heaven. Instead she made the gross error of remarking at once 'Ee-jow-ee-jow! I-yam-a-very-good-girl! No-body-is-as-clever-as-me! Ee-jow-ee-jow-ee-jow-ee-jow!'—which, taking into account the smug and self-admiring rictus which still adorned her stupid face, was enough to get her taken down to the sandpit and crucified all over again. Eventually her arms fell off under this treatment but as we had not yet finished with the game we sewed her a new pair on, made out of brown ribbed stockings.

Thomas, our father, was scandalised by our barbarity and wanted to forbid it, but our mother stopped him on psychological grounds. 'Don't make it seem too important!' she said, 'That might fix it! Let it wear itself out!' Which of course, in a week or two, it did.

Thomas himself used to play a game when he was a child that had an element of destruction in it. He would raid the basket of kindling where chips of wood, all cloven and chopped to the same size, lay ready for the lighting of the morning's fires. He would take a good bundle, and painstakingly build them up into a little house like a log cabin, with a door opening, and windows, and a roof all neatly thatched with straw. And then he

10

would set fire to it and watch it burn down . . . luckily nobody stopped him or did anything to 'fix it'. It would have been terrible to have a father who was an arsonist.

After we had quelled Violet and moved on to other things the crucifixion motif fell into desuetude in our house and it was Papa, our grandfather, who next raised the subject, many years later. It was just after the war, and we had a new gardener. His name was Windle, and he had received his early training in the household of a nobleman whom it might be as well to refer to as Lord Blahbrough. Windle was a delightful man as well as a knowledgeable gardener and we all enjoyed chatting to him as he worked about the borders. It was after one of these chats that Papa strolled into the house and remarked 'You know, Windle is a most interesting man. He was telling me that when he was at Lord Blahbrough's he took part in Stainer's "Crucifixion" '—an observation which inspired Thomas to go away and write a little poem, only the first verse of which has survived. It went:

'Windle!' Lord Blahbrough said one day
To his best-loved retainer—
'We've nothing much to do—I say!
Let's crucify old Stainer!'

Luckily for us our parents were not religious and although we were subjected to holy influences at Miss Allen's school there were no attempts to send us to church or to Sunday School. Religion being thus shorn of its boring, dutiful aspect appeared to us in the nature of a drama and a mystery, and religious ceremonies of one kind and another formed the basis of many of our games. We buried things, of course; all children do—the goldfish Percy, a chance dead mouse, a bird caught by the cat— but we did it with a good deal of style with the burial service read sonorously by Richard, wreaths of daisies by the grave, and a tin cigarette box for a coffin. Richard's sacerdotal wear was his dressing gown, put on back to front, and a white table napkin which peeped over the top in a very fair imitation of a dog-collar. The hearse was a little blue cart, drawn by an exceedingly attractive animal called Horsy. His basic construction was of wood, but he was covered with a harsh brown fur something

11

like thin carpet in texture, and in his battered countenance sparkled two brilliant, knowing black eyes. Moved along in little jumps by the parson he did his job well enough on the flat, but the coffin always fell out of the hearse on the way down the Little Hill, and the funeral procession would pause at the foot to regroup and give the mourners a chance to shake the levity out of their systems.

We went to church once. We prevailed on nurse to take us to morning service and we all listened like anything in the hope of picking up fresh material for our religious games. I was soon lost, flicking the pages between matins and the psalms in a fog of bewilderment, but Richard got some good bits. 'You must not say the beastly spirit, for I mean to mean', he would intone thereafter, and vow, if challenged, that those were the very words he had heard the vicar say.

Our parents were having their after-lunch coffee one day when they were favoured by a visitation in the name of religion. Richard came first. He opened the dining-room door—wearing his priestly robes—and announced in thrilling tones 'He's Coming!' (you could hear the capitals in his voice). I was 'He' on that occasion and I treated it frivolously, wearing a sheet and an exiguous blond beard, and wielding a broken fairy wand with which I made passes at my elders as I capered about. But Richard was magnificent. All through the performance he stood by the door with head bowed and hands palm to palm, as in prayer. And while 'He' skipped in haste round the table and out of the door again Richard cried out like a saint in a vision 'Holy! Holy! Holy!'

The beard which I donned as part of my Messianic disguise came from a make-up box, which was one of the most successful presents that Thomas and Elspeth ever gave us. It was stage make-up, greasepaint, with eyeshadow and lipstick and rouge and black eyepencil, and a little bottle of glue, with false hair in enough colours to make even Nick Bottom green with envy. We loved it. At first we just messed around with it and stuck beards and moustaches on to our faces for the fun of it, but it did suggest theatre and before long we began to make up and perform little plays in the nursery. Our audience was composed of conscripts, to wit Nurse, Ardar (the secretary), the maids, our parents, and any partners who might be unlucky enough to be in the house at the time of the performance.

Our best effort was 'Orpheus and Eurydice'. The costumes, being drapey and classical, were contrived from old sheets, and there was a good chance for beards in the parts of Pluto and Orpheus. There was only one problem—the serpent. In the legend Eurydice gets bitten by a serpent in the very first bit of the action, and a serpent was one of the things we just did not have. An exploratory mission that thought to cut a bit off the car-washing hose-pipe was forestalled and firmly ridden off by Yeadon, the gardener, so we retired in disorder to the nursery for a further consultation. We were fairly stumped.

It was Gillian who found it in the end, while rummaging for sheets in the patching drawer—a mysterious object that seemed custom built for our purpose, although we had no idea what its true function might be. It was a length of rubber tubing, thin and bright red, with a white nozzle on one end that, as Gillian said, was quite like the thing on a rattlesnake's tail. It swelled out in the middle quite a lot and we thought that would do for a head, though we know that the best serpents kept their heads at one end and not in the middle. But that was after all but a detail. We painted a good big pair of staring eyes and a forked tongue on to the central swelling and reckoned we were lucky to have found it. It really was very effective. If somebody off stage coiled it up very tightly and threw it onto the ground near Eurydice it bounced around very convincingly, and we hoped that its anatomical defects would be obscured in this flurry of activity. We thought it was fine.

But even so we were somewhat taken aback by the enormous burst of applause that greeted its entry. Our largely medical audience were delighted with it, and the venemous enema was decidely the star of the show. It was a pity it was all in the first scene, though; the rest of the action rather dragged in comparison.

When I look back on our life in the nursery it seems hard to realize that it was as recent as the nineteen thirties. Things were so different then that it might have been in another age. Where nowadays could you lean out of the window as we would to admire a funeral, drawn up by the church just across the road

13

where the hearse was drawn by six black horses with black ostrich feather plumes between their ears and splendid silver-trimmed black harness? Where could you find a hurdy-gurdy man (only we called it a tinkelairy) who would come as a matter of course whenever he was passing and play for you for ten minutes in your own yard? We used to throw down pennies to him, and he would bob down and pick them up off the floor and smile up at us with broken, discoloured teeth before trundling his tinkelairy off down the road leaving our ears ringing with the plangent strains of 'Two lovely black eyes' or 'Under the lilacs she twanged her guitar', or Nurse's favourite 'Drive home James, and don't spare the horses'.

Another anachronism was the muffin man who would materialise out of the dusk of a November afternoon ringing a handbell to advertise the delicious wares which he carried on a tray slung round his neck, covered with a white cloth. The youngest maid would be sent out with a shilling to chaffer with him, and then we would all have crumpets for tea, or pikelets, which were much the same only a bit smaller.

Children's parties were another thing that seem in retrospect to be almost 'period'. One wore the most delightful clothes for them. From a very early age little girls had long dresses and I used to wait with bated breath for Gillian to grow out of certain coveted frocks so that I could inherit them. One I remember was of flame-coloured taffeta with a tucked skirt banded with tiny edgings of palest blue. Another which I never did succeed to, being thwarted by the war, was of pale spring-green net, with a delicate ruched bodice. With these one wore bronze dancing pumps with ribbon rosettes on them, and cross-over elastics, white socks with clocks, and, to go and come back in, long velvet cloaks that fastened at the neck. Little boys wore suits of navy serge or grey flannel with rather long short trousers, well-pulled-up and gartered grey socks, patent leather shoes, and brilliantined hair. Our performance at parties when we were very young was always marred by a pathological hatred of balloons which were forced upon you, all unwilling, by kindly do-gooding hostesses and helpers until you burst into hysterical tears and rushed away to hide yourself behind the long velvet curtains in the dining room thus missing not only the conjuror and the games of 'oranges and lemons' with prizes, but the polka and the gallop at the end, which you all knew how to do, having all been taught it at the same dancing class on Saturday mornings.

Going out for walks with one's nurse is an activity that seems to have faded out of the lives of the middle classes, but it was *de rigueur* in our day. Buttoned into your leggings with a buttonhook if the weather was cold and in any case always decently coated and gloved, you set forth each day for the statutory hour's perambulation on any one of half a dozen routes. Every one was studded with good bits and bad bits, codified by long familiarity and enjoyed equally for the never-failing response they evoked. There was the warehouse we were frightened of where a pulley with a pair of terrible claws on a chain hung over the path. They were really for raising wool bales with, but we had a kind of technical fear-response every time we saw them and would never walk directly under them. Then there was the 'pretty birds' bit where the path flanked a private aviary in which some golden and silver pheasants pecked dispiritedly at the bare-trodden, soot-blackened ground. There was the canal with the big noble bulk of the gasworks with its gasometers, its heaps of coke, and its almost palpable aura of smell hanging round it in a cloud. It was exciting to walk along the canal. Narrow boats pulled by horses sometimes passed and you could watch the brawny, red-armed women from them opening the swing bridge to let them through; or a dead dog, bloated, feet in the air, might float slowly and majestically past, finding its own way from Leeds to Liverpool.

Sometimes Nurse took us on these walks and sometimes Elspeth did, and then we went further afield, for we would start in her little Austin 7 car and drive a bit, and then walk in more unfamiliar fields and lanes. Occasionally we were taken to see special things like the Hindenburg. I remember standing waiting on a hill somewhere when this was due to pass and then seeing it, a brilliant silvery little cigar, high in the sky, floating along so silently and so purposefully. Another time Elspeth irrupted quite unexepectedly into the nursery and plucked us all coatless from our play to be whisked off to see the strange sight of a covered wagon with a full team of eight oxen plodding

15

its way slowly along the Leeds and Bradford road, advertising tea or suet or oranges or something long forgotten. 'I don't suppose you'll ever see anything like that again in your lives', she said, and so far at least she has been right—I haven't, anyway.

Nurse was with us through all our early childhood, but after she left and before we all went away to school there was a disagreeable interregnum when we were committed to the care of a young Swiss nursery-governess called Simone.

I don't know why, but we hated Simone from the beginning. We averred that she had large hairy hands like a man's and we made up a simple song which we sang in her absence, to the tune of one of Sousa's most rousing marches. It went:

> Simone rubs her hairy hands with glee,
> Simone rubs her hairy hands with glee,
> She *rubs* her *hairy* hands,
> She *rubs* her *hairy* hands,
> She rubs her hands with glee.

She was supposed to teach us French; a more thankless task can never have been undertaken in the whole course of human education. It was approached entirely through vocabulary; grammar was, perhaps fortunately, left to shift for itself. We were meant to commit about ten words a week to memory, and Thomas would test us on them every Saturday afternoon. The prize for the winner was threepence, stacked temptingly in view on the black marble dining room mantlepiece. But we resented the whole business and fell back on the age old defence that is the strongest available to the weaker party—sulky non-co-operation. We did not dare to say 'I don't know' too many times when Thomas, with kindling wrath held in check by a great effort of self-control, asked us over and over again each week 'What is the French for "chair"? or "table"? or "school"?' We just made sure we always got it wrong, and eventually our persistent sabotage had the desired effect and the French tests were dropped. I once incurred the wrath of the other two by accidentally getting a word right. The threepence was immediately handed over with a few comments to the others to the effect that if the youngest could do so well, didn't they think they could . . . et cetera. I

16

had a hard job convincing them that my resounding success was due to absence of mind rather than disloyalty; indeed, I was ostracised for two or three hours, and only really succeeded in buying my way back into favour by spending the threepence on sweets and dividing them out.

But perhaps even more than the French tests it was the dreadful affair of 'Lepperteenardo' that turned us against Simone. I don't know whether it was Elspeth's suggestion that we should perform a little French song, 'with actions', to the assembled grown-ups at Christmas, or whether Simone devised the idea from the sadistic depths of her own black soul; but somehow the plan took root and, drag our feet as we might, we were propelled ruthlessly along the path to what we felt was the crowning humiliation of the performance. It was not that we were stage-shy; far from it—we had been producing and writing our own plays in the nursery for years. But this was different. I suppose, although we didn't know the word at the time, we must have thought it was 'wet', but resistance was in vain. The whole might of the adult world was ranged against us; Miss Maud, our piano teacher, oversaw the musical side, Elspeth made terrible costumes of casement cloth in various colours, and Simone herself both dragooned us through the choreography and dinned the words into us with such ferocity that I remember them still. They do not, it is true, bear a very striking resemblance to the tongue of Racine and Molière, but nevertheless, this is what we sang, resentfully pushing imaginary besoms about the drawing room carpet on the afternoon of Christmas day:

> Lepperteenardo la montineyer—
> There do your netter, there do your
> Lan wee fer tooter la bersonyer,
> Porduck a dormuck la berjay.

There was a lot more of it; it is easy to see that it was all quite unforgivable. But fortunately Simone was only engaged for a year, and when her time was up, went gladly back to Switzerland, while we reverted to the much more congenial company of the maids.

TWO

THE MAIDS

When I read in Kenneth Clark's autobiography about how disagreeable the servants were to him, I felt very sorry, because our experience was so totally different. No doubt our servants were different too—of a different order. We kept two maids to do the cooking and the housework and of course, over the years, a good many spent some time with us; usually they came from the South Yorkshire coalfields. They arrived at fourteen, straight from school, and usually stayed with us until they left to get married at eighteen or twenty. Occasionally we had an older one like Lily, who used to warn threateningly 'I'll saw yer leg off', or Myra, who drank vinegar straight from the bottle and became very yellow and shrewish, but the average complement was one of fifteen and one of seventeen, and the cosy, firelit kitchen made a pleasant alternative to the nursery.

There was never any constraint between the maids and the children. I imagine that they all came from large families, and felt that a scattering of young children underfoot was a normal, comfortable fact of life. Sometimes a maid like Joan, who lived reasonably close, would take us to her home for tea. We went as far as Bradford on the trolley bus or trackless tram, usually referred to as the 'trackless', *tout court*. I always spelled it tracklass in my mind's eye which gave it a dashing, faintly nautical air—by association, presumably, with windlass and cutlass. We stayed on the tracklass till the end of its run and lingered to watch it turning round. The driver made a three-point turn and the conductor stood in the road and poked the thing that was connected to the overhead cables into its new position, with an enormously long pole. Showers of sparks shot out, with great fizzings and splutterings, and a noticeable smell of ozone filled the air; it was like a Guy Fawkes night in miniature.

We did the last bit of our journey in a lorry driven by a

brother, who picked us up at the tracklass stop. We had never been in a lorry before, and we were awed by the height off the ground, the thunderous din of its engine, and the smell, like coarse, damp sacks, that pervaded its cab. We had chattered away briskly enough on the tracklass but now, closely packed in with the big strange brother, we fell silent and only smiled, shyly.

We went on being shy, too, at first, when we got to our destination. The kitchen was small and brilliantly lit. An enormous coal fire burned in the range, and the room seemed to be full of people. To tell the truth, we were something of a curiosity to the people of that district and several neighbours had taken a chance of dropping in to have a look at us.

But Joan's mother was so kind that nobody could stay shy for long with her. She called us all 'loov' and sat us down at the loaded table where we feasted on rare delicacies like tinned salmon and tinned peaches with evaporated milk poured over them. We never had that at home. With the five of us (our Ramsden cousins Bruce and Judith were with us) and Joan sitting round the table it was pretty well filled up, but the neighbours found seats around the room and drank cups of strong tea, thick with condensed milk. One woman had a baby of about a year old which was evidently just beginning to talk. 'Tea!' it said, climbing upright on its mother's lap and plucking at her dress. 'Tea-tea-tea-tea-tea!' 'I think perhaps it wants a cup of tea', said Gillian helpfully. A ripple of amusement passed over the group of women. 'Nay, love', said the mother. 'That's not what 'e said.' Whereupon to our consternation she unbuttoned her blouse and produced a vast purplish breast, onto which the infant fastened with loud animal noises of delight. 'There you are!' she said. 'Titty, that's what 'e wanted'. We were abashed, and looked down at our plates.

Before long the men began to arrive back from their shift at the pit. Several of them—the father, with two or three grown-up sons—clattered in on nailed boots and threw their snap-tins down on the side table. They looked amazing. They were still in their pit muck, and their pale eyes gleamed pinkish, like ferrets' eyes, out of their black faces. They grinned broadly when they saw us, and their big white teeth flashed brilliantly as they

19

shouted loud pleasantries at us in the broadest of broad Yorkshire. It was difficult to know what to say in reply because none
of us could understand a word they were saying. 'I'm afraid I
don't speak French', said four-year-old Bruce politely to one of
these sallies—an answer that brought the house down.

We were tired by the time we got back to the tracklass, and
we leaned against Joan on the way home. But we had enjoyed it;
sheltered by our privileged position as visitors, somewhat petted
and spoiled, we had looked at a different world, as marine ex-
plorers in a bathyscaphe peer out at the seething, fleeing, devouring shoals around them. Janet and Joan were at home in that
world; they could enter it at will without any need of a protective
bathyscaphe. They could deal with the situations as they arose—
prepare the baths in the wash-house for the returning colliers
and understand and cap their broad badinage—or seize a crying,
spewing baby and deftly knock the wind up out of it before
whipping its nappy off and changing it. We wouldn't have
swopped our cool, spacious house for their seething, struggling
existence; but we felt their naturalness and their vigour all the
same. What we peered at through our protective glass globe in
those colliers' terraced houses was LIFE, raw, raucous and fertile;
and our maids knew all about it.

People who lived in that fierce medium of LIFE (as opposed to
people like us who were somewhat detached) seemed to be
swept along by it like straws in a mighty rushing torrent. The
particular current in which our maids were swirling was the
rapids of sex. They were totally preoccupied with it. It filled
their lives, dominated their imaginations, and coloured their
dreams, as if they were bulling heifers. Like the undergraduate
in the old joke they never thought of anything else. And being
basically coarse girls, they thought about it in a coarse way. But
somehow you couldn't really take exception to it. It was so
obviously beyond their own volition. It was the LIFE in them,
having its way.

John Moore saw the continuity between the villagers of
Brensham and the country characters in Shakespeare, but our
maids reached further back than that; they could have stepped
from the pages of Chaucer. To them, sex was not only an intense
preoccupation—it was also a joke—a great big rich glorious

20

hearty bottom-smacking sort of joke at which you roared with laughter even while you entered into it with gusto. Nothing was sacred. Romantic love was not even hinted at, and anything could be 'told'; everything was. We were fascinated by it all, although some instinct warned us that it wouldn't do to mention it to the 'grown-ups'. Ours was not a prurient interest either, in spite of the secrecy, but a kind of uproarious innocent pleasure of knowledge that I didn't meet again until I recognised it in the immortal Geoffrey.

'He swyved thee—yea, algates, in it went!' The language may be fourteenth century, but the spirit of earthy frankness is just as I remember it in the long evenings when we got our education, sitting in a row on the rag rug in front of the fire in the East Gate kitchen.

It was a homely room. About twenty feet square, its two big sash windows looked out onto the yard and the Lombardy poplars in which you could see a barn-owl roosting. A good fire always glowed in the big black range; the hearth, stoned to snowy white-ness, was protected by a bright steel fender that had to be rubbed up with steel wool. There was a flat round bit in the middle, right in front of and below the raised fire, where Boots, our tortoiseshell cat, loved to lie. One day a red-hot cinder rolled out of the fire and fell onto her back and she rushed, screaming, three or four times round the room with it sticking to her singeing fur before we could catch her to flick it off. She was dressed with tannic acid jelly from the surgery, and healed up in a week or two.

There were two big scrubbed deal tables in the kitchen, one in the middle and one against the wall beneath one of the windows, and to me they were symbols of all that makes a home more than a house. They were always in use for something or other. Pastry was rolled out on them; newspapers were spread on them for brass- and silver-cleaning; or, in the evenings, the ironing blanket was spread out on the middle one, and one maid ironed while the other one sat in the old Windsor chair by the fire, and we sat on the rag rug by the fender, and we all talked.

Janet's iron pushed rhythmically across the ironing blanket, smoothing out shirts, sheets, pillow cases and handkerchiefs, while the pleasant singey smell filled the kitchen. The pile of rolled-up damp clothes in the big wicker washing basket shrank

21

steadily, and the pulley, which we called a creel, let down by the fire, grew heavier and heavier with the freshly-ironed garments that were laid carefully across its bars.

We did not talk against a background of silence. Wireless had not yet penetrated into our simple household, but there was a gramaphone and a case of records. They were 78's of course, thick, heavy and fragile, and you wound the gramophone up and changed the needle from a supply in a little oblong tin with a picture of the H.M.V. dog on the lid. Used needles were put into a little triangular tray that you could press out from the corner of the gramophone box itself, which seemed to concentrate in itself all the essence of the authentic gramophone smell. One whiff of that smell recalls instantly all the songs we used to play —Layton and Johnston, 'The Bam-bam-bammy shore'; 'Two Black Crows'; 'Underneath the Arches' with Flanagan and Allan; 'The Sunday Drivers'; and Fred and Adèle Astaire with 'I'd rather Charleston', 'Fascinatin' rhythm' and 'I've got the you don't know the half of it dearie blues'.

Inside the lid of the record box was a message printed by Thomas in exasperated capitals giving instructions on the proper use of the gramophone: 'PLEASE, PLEASE, FOR GOD'S SAKE HANDLE THESE RECORDS CAREFULLY' it began, and finished off 'IF YOU ARE NATURALLY CLUMSY OR CARELESS, GET SOMEBODY ELSE TO OPERATE THE MACHINE FOR YOU'. I thought it was funny, but I don't think the maids had ever even noticed it.

To these tunes we heard the latest plans in Janet the junior maid's campaign to ensnare the postman, and followed the triumphant progress of Joan the elder one's affair with her 'young man', which had got to a more solid, biological stage. The act of love was always described by the maids as 'Joining' which made it difficult for us to control our giggles when pompous uncles said things like 'Shall we join the ladies?' Bruce once knowingly drew our attention to a joiner's shop when we were all driving along in his father's car, but he was taken aback when everybody remained absolutely stony-faced at this piece of wit. He was younger than the rest of us and had not then absorbed the first rule of conduct, which was never, never, never risk anything you're not sure about in the presence of the grown-ups.

But even though we knew better than to mention joining anywhere except the kitchen, we thought it was quite a fascinating idea. It was a long time before we realised that it was not an exclusively human activity, and I remember quite a flash of enlightenment when, at the age of seven or so, I began to read books about nature, and realised that flowers and bees and things carried on just like people.

While we were more or less *au fait* with the physical mechanics of 'joining', we remained totally ignorant of its social connotations, and it never occurred to us that it was an activity that called for suitability of both time and place. This caused substantial disappointment one afternoon when John, Joan's young man, came to the house to tea. It wasn't exactly that we expected him to leap upon her in our presence and bear her down to the kitchen floor, but we did think that at least something might have transpired in the course of the afternoon. We were there when he arrived, a blue-chinned, razor-nicked young miner with great red hands and thick wrists, and he didn't even kiss her. He shuffled into the kitchen, inarticulate as a dog, and sat on the very edge of his chair, dangling his flat cap between his knees and clearing his throat. From time to time he produced a comb from his breast pocket and sleeked back his quiffed, Brylcreemed hair. Conversation was stilted.

'These are t'children I've bin tellin' yer about, John.'

'Oh aye?'

'This is Gillian—this is Richard—and Libby's t'little 'un.'

'Oh aye?'

We shook his great fist politely, but it was hard to equate this hangdog hobbledehoy with the virile, passionate lover of Joan's description. We sat in a row on the table waiting for a bit of action, but he remained disappointingly inert.

'Do you think she could possibly have been making it all up?' asked Richard when we had finally withdrawn, unfulfilled.

'Oh no, I'm sure it's true' said Gillian. 'After all, Janet says so too. But he seems terribly shy.'

Eventually we decided that that being so, he probably needed a bit of special encouragement. So we went into the surgery and, purloining a couple of sheets of medicine-bottle wrapping paper, we printed appropriate messages on them with the scratchy

23

surgery pen. JOINING read one banner, succinctly, while the other declared JOHN PULL'S JOAN'S KNICKERS DOWN. Then, since the kitchen windows were some way above the ground, we impaled these on long bamboos and paraded to and fro in the yard for some minutes in the hope that the reluctant swain might catch a glimpse and realise what was expected of him. We were so convulsed by now by our own wit and daring that I don't think we held the notices very straight—and this, added to the straggliness of our three-inch capitals, probably saved him from the terrible embarrassment of guessing what we were up to. Suffice to say that our efforts didn't have the blighting effect that one might have expected; a year or so later Joan left to marry John and one must hope they lived as happy ever after as most people do.

Our parents would have had a fit if they had realised the hand that the maids were taking in the education of their children, but I don't think our premature knowledge really did us any harm. They were silly girls, certainly; they were coarse and ignorant; but they were perfectly natural, and above all they had the great saving grace of being warm-hearted. That was one of the reasons we enjoyed being in the kitchen—you felt that they liked you.

They were amazingly credulous. Once in a game of 'Truth or Dare' Joan dared Janet to drink a whole cupful of Epsom salts, a feat which Janet performed with insouciance. 'Bananas 'll stop yer,' she said. 'A banana 'll stop anything.' So she nipped into the dining room and took one from the fruit bowl and although I forgot to ask her the next day if it had worked I presume it must have, for she certainly didn't look any different from usual.

All our maids were terrified of thunder and the lurid glare of an impending storm sent them scuttling about like ants in a disturbed nest. There were various things in the house that could 'draw' lightning and these had to be dealt with according to their kind. All windows had to be shut, not so much to keep out the rain, but because lightning might sneak in at an open window—everybody knew that. Mirrors were either turned round to face the wall or draped with dust sheets, as were any pictures with glass. Finally any piece of silver was put away, and the cutlery drawer firmly shut, for silver 'drew' lightning more than all the rest put together. When all the preparations were

24

made we got together in the kitchen and sat out the storm, keeping up our spirits with big slices of delicious bread and dripping until the thunder rolled away and the sky shone lemon-pale once more behind the wet stone roofs.

As well as being superstitious, the maids were purveyors of ghastly stories about illnesses and accidents. One concerned a little boy who got appendicitis, but didn't tell his mother. 'And then 'is bowels burst, and everything floated up (illustrated by a hideously expressive wavering motion of the hands) and 'e died in agony.' This made a terrible impression on Richard, and for months when Elspeth had come up to kiss us goodnight and turn the lights off you would hear an anxious little voice calling out of his bedroom 'Mummy, do you think my bowels will burst tonight?'

The reason for the kitchen windows being so high above the yard was that the house had a complete cellar underneath it, and in some places, according to the tilt of the land, a little bit of the cellar windows came above ground level. The part of the cellar that extended under the kitchen was the washkitchen. You entered it from outside down some steep steps which led down to the coal cellar (which had two stalls, one full of kitchen coal, the other with great lumps of 'Derby Brights' for the drawing and dining rooms). Skirting the coal, you passed through another door, and found yourself in a large room about twenty feet square, dimly lit by two north-facing windows, only the top panes of which were above ground level. Most of the cellar windows were like this, each with its little stone area and a heavy metal grating to stop you falling down it.

The washing equipment was built on the same homeric scale as the washkitchen itself. A great big copper stood in one corner; and most of the rest of that wall was taken up with a big black grate, with two hobs. Solid slab stone shelves ran round the side walls, to hold things like the starch, the soap and the dolly blue. A large flat stone sink stood under one window, and the rest of the equipment—mangles, peggy tubs, and all the rest of it—stood around in appointed places on the floor.

Mrs Box, our washerwoman, was big and strong, with black, gypsy curls, and a square, yellowish face. Her arms, bare,

25

muscular, and usually flecked with suds, were pale and lightly freckled all over. I don't know whether she washed for other people on other days of the week; she came to us every Monday, and one week's washing for all of us took her most of the day to complete. We were, of course, quite a big household. As well as the five of us who made up the family, there were Nurse and two maids—not to mention any visitors.

Mrs Box arrived early on washdays, and her first job was to fill the copper, and get the two fires going. While the water was warming, she brought down the dirty linen, sorted it, and put the whites to soak. They went in a peggy tub, in warm soapy water. The soap was yellow and hard and came in long bars, square in section. It was grated into the water on the coarse side of an ordinary kitchen grater, and swirled round until it dissolved. The source of hot water in many washkitchens was the copper, but ours had the amenity of a hot tap plumbed down from the kitchen, with great lengths of loopy, crazy-looking pipe, roughly lagged with felt.

There was a very special atmosphere in the washkitchen. Clouds of steam filled the air and diffused the different areas of light—the grey light from the windows, the yellow nimbus around the single naked lamp bulb, and the ruddy glow from the two fires, whose glowing embers spilled red reflections onto the wet stone floor. Mrs Box moved here and there, massive and purposeful, ladling clothes from the soak into the copper to boil, rubbing, rinsing, starching, and bluing, while the smell of the coal fire, the damp whitewashed walls, the yellow soap and the clean linen swept and billowed around her.

The actual washing process was hard work. You took the next heap of clothes, sorted according to priorities, and dropped them into the peggy tub of hot suds. Then you 'possed' them vigorously for a few minutes. The posser was a thing like an inverted colander on a straight wooden handle, and you pushed the clothes up and down with it until they were thoroughly wetted and soapy. Then you reached for the dolly. This was like a small, stout milking-stool, with a handle growing straight up out of the seat. The handle had a cross-piece, and as you held it by this and twisted to and fro, the clothes were agitated in the same way as in a modern washing machine. But this was not the end of your manual involvement. In Yorkshire at any rate, spotless washing was a matter of great pride, so, discarding your dolly, you stood a rubbing board in the tub, and scrubbed the garments briskly up and down its ridges until your arm was ready to drop off.

Then you mangled. We had two mangles in the washkitchen —one a great big thing with wooden rollers nearly a foot in diameter, and the other smaller, on a metal stand. Both were turned by a handle at the side, and it was quite hard work, on the big one at least. Everything had two or three rinses, with manglings between, and was then finished off with starch or bluebag or both according to kind.

I liked both starch and bluebag. Mrs Box had a big earthenware bowl like a bread bowl, red outside and yellow inside, for mixing the starch in, and she boiled up a big black iron kettle on the fire to make it. I loved to see the thin white paste turn magically to the clear, pale blue starch as she deftly poured in the stream of boiling water with one hand and stirred with the other, while fresh clouds of sweet-scented steam rose into the air.

Bluebag was even nicer. When they were new, the little muslin bags, tied up round a wooden peg with a sort of head on it, looked just like little country milkmaids—without arms, it is true, but sweetly buxom and dimity-looking. They were rather draggled when they had performed their function of bluing the rinses, and they had lost their pleasing plumpness and symmetry; but we were allowed to have them then, and once they had dried out they made very suitable inhabitants for the doll's house.

The washing was dried, weather permitting, in the yard. It was a big yard, with a high stone wall and a row of Lombardy poplars in front of it. Outside the stables an area of cobbled 'setts' sloping down to a central drain was where they used to wash the carriages when the house was built in 1860. The old well was there, too, covered with a stone slab. It still had water in it, but it was a long way down—you waited and waited when you dropped a pebble in until the flat, echoing 'plunk' told you that it had reached the bottom.

The clothes lines were stretched between the poplars and the house, and Mrs Box carried up creaking wash baskets full of wet linen and pegged it out in the fine flapping breeze. Shirts bosomed out; sheets swelled like spinnakers; stockings danced a

27

mad jig. And when it was dry, it all had to be folded up, smelling of fresh air, and brought into the kitchen to be 'sprinkled'. When it was all tightly rolled up and damped ready for ironing, Mrs Box's work was done, and she would sit for a while in the kitchen massively relaxed, like a statue by Henry Moore, over a last cup of tea before she gathered up her things and went home.

Mrs Box was the last washerwoman to use all the old-fashioned equipment at East Gate. After she left, Elspeth advertised for a replacement, and a very nice woman applied for the job.

'But you'll 'ave ter get me an electric washing machine first,' she added firmly.

Elspeth was 'fair capped'. 'But if I've got a washing machine, I don't need a washerwoman, do I?' she essayed.

'Ee, loov' replied the woman gently. 'That isn't the 'arf of it. And what I think is that it seems wrong that a woman should 'ave to spend all day down there labouring—aye, labouring away until the sweat runs down 'er back, when there's a machine that'll do most of the hard bit for 'er. And you can afford one, you know, loov.'

'And when I thought about it in those terms,' said Elspeth, 'I could see that she was absolutely right. So I did buy a washing machine, and she did do the washing for a bit, but then her husband changed his job, and she moved out of the district, so I lost her. And then of course the war came, and I was glad then that I had got the washing machine. It did very well.'

Another regular visitor to our kitchen or, at least, to the little lobby which separated it from the back door, was our very charming milkman, who was always extremely friendly to us children.

It is difficult to realise that in the 1930s we had three deliveries of milk a day at East Gate. The middle one was from a very modern local farm called Cotelands, and the milk was Grade A tuberculin tested, in bottles, for us children to drink. Grade A caused me some problems. I have always had a mind that will opt for the wrong end of any stick that is offered it, and for years I thought it was a kind of milk peculiar to Cotelands Farm and that Grey Day was a sort of brand name—a suitably cool, fresh, non-souring kind of image, after all. It wasn't only the milk that

28

caused my mind to boggle. I also interpreted amiss the line in the hymn which declares 'Fading is the worldlings' pleasure', and dimly pictured the worldlings saying to one another things like 'Coming down to my place for a quick fade on Saturday?' or 'Harry and I enjoyed some absolutely splendid fading after you'd left yesterday'. Another hymn was even more puzzling because the copies we had of the words, made on the school copying machine had a misprint which read 'Ye behold him fac to face'. The music mistress, referring to this, said 'Of course I don't need to tell you what that should really be, do I?' Oh fatal lack of clarity! For some reason I instantly rejected the obvious and concluded it must be something tremendously esoteric, a phrase in Sanskrit perhaps, meaning something like back to front—which, obviously, everybody who *was* anybody knew about without being told, but which I had somehow missed out on.

The other two deliveries of milk were brought to our house by a local milkman called Mr Bell. He was a small, spare man with dark twinkling eyes, weatherbeaten red cheeks, and a hooky nose, his general air being rather like that of Mr Punch. He drove a milk float, pulled by a pony that was exactly the colour of milk chocolate, and which bit. It used to stand with its front feet up on the pavement, laying back its ears and flaring its wicked eyes behind its blinkers as it lunged with open mouth at unwary passers by. Once, seeing it grazing in its field, and having some oats in my pocket I decided to pay it a visit to try and win its confidence. The result was exceedingly ignominious. It let me walk right up to it in the middle of the field, then bared its yellow teeth and chased me back to the road making loud snapping noises an inch behind my scuttling posterior.

Mr Bell's milk did not come in bottles. Instead, he had an oval milk can with a lid, made of some silvery metal, but with hinges and fastenings of brass. Different measures—gill, half pint and pint—hung inside the can in the milk on long curved handles that hooked over the rim; you took your jug to the back door, and Mr Bell measured the exact amount into it, and then gave you a little drop more for good measure. Then you took the milk down into the cellar to keep cool, for there were no refrigerators in the average house in those days. While the milk was standing around in its jug, there was always the risk that a fly might fall in and drown, so you protected it by thowing a little net cover over it, weighted all round the edge with lovely clear blue glass beads. These things, like kettle holders, came in very handy as presents for your female relations that you could make at a very early age and that actually were useful.

We liked Mr Bell. He always seemed to have time for a chat, and when he was in a good mood he would sing to us. One of his songs was a traditional one:

> One fine day in the middle of the night
> Two dead men got up to fight.
> One blind man to see fair play,
> Two deaf and dumb men to shout 'hooray';
> A paralysed donkey passing by
> Kicked the blind man in the eye,
> Sent him spinning through a nine-inch wall
> Into a dry ditch and drowned them all.

We enjoyed this song, which we considered had some very subtle touches, but the other one was even better, because it was filthy. Mr Bell would only sing it occasionally, and then in a specially quiet voice and leaning forward, so we all had to crowd round conspiratorially. It was very short:

> One fine day in the middle of the night
> Three dead tom-cats got up to fight
> One had a fiddle, the other had a drum,
> And the other had a pancake strapped to his bum.

One day Thomas decided that it was hardly fair for the entertainment to be so one-sided, so he wrote us a little song to sing in reply. The tune was quite a well-known one, and it went:

> Good morning, Mr Bell, Bell, Bell,
> You are certainly a-looking fine.
> Good morning, Mr Bell, Bell, Bell,
> Get your hair cut just as short as mine—
> Ashes to ashes and dust to dust,
> If the milking doesn't tire you then delivering must—

Good morning, Mr Bell, Bell, Bell,
You are certainly a-looking
         certainly a-looking
         certainly a-looking fine!

So thereafter we used to stand in a solemn row and exchange
these ritual greetings whenever we didn't happen to be at school.

THREE

MISS ALLEN'S

I was three when I started school. Everybody acknowledged that
it was a bit young, but Richard and Gillian were both going,
and it appears that I made such a fuss at being left behind that
they sent me along for the sake of peace and quiet.

The school was about a hundred yards away from our house,
right-handed down at the leafy, quiet end of the street, opposite
the church. If you turned left at our gate instead and walked up
the hill, life became a lot more dangerous. It is true that a series
of large houses with verdurous, secluded gardens occupied the
left-hand side of the road; but opposite a number of streets ran
off at right angles to the road, streets whose names followed the
letters of the alphabet, Arthur, Bertha, Clara, Donald; and where
there should have been Edmund or Elvin or Ellen, there was
Francis Street, which was given a double helping of territory in
order to accommodate a truly terrifying council school. Ragged
children swarmed, yelling, in its playground, lining the railings
to shout incomprehensible abuse at us, and I am sure that they
would have attacked us if we had not always been convoyed by
Nurse. It was one of Thomas's most effective threats to say, when
we were particularly tiresome, 'I don't know why I bother to
spend all this money on your education. You might as well go to
Francis Street and be done with it.' We always became instantly
amenable under that suggestion.

Our own school was really a church school, but was always
referred to by the name of its only mistress, as 'Miss Allen's'.
Miss Allen herself was quite a character. She was the eldest of
four sisters, all of whom had remained unmarried, and lived with
their mother. The chief characteristic of the whole family was
that they were 'ladies'. Each member of it seemed to epitomise
some particular tenet of ladylikeness, as if she had been born
with it tucked in her mouth like a cracker motto; thus Miss Alice

(our Miss Allen) illustrated the fact that 'A lady does not raise her voice': Miss Maud, who came to the house to give us piano lessons, that 'A lady meets all disagreeable circumstances with a brave and cheerful demeanour', and Miss Madge and Miss Violet that 'A lady never goes out without her hat or gloves, or laughs in a public place'. All four of them had gentle, well-modulated voices and exquisitely correct accents, as indeed had the old lady. she was an old lady, too—very old. 'My mother,' Miss Allen sometimes told us with pride, 'is so old that her eyesight has come back to her.' What can she have meant? I have often pondered over it. The only explanation that I can think of is that she must have had a successful operation for cataract.

Another thing that Miss Allen once said I can find no explanation for at all. Beaming with her special brand of religious goodness, she remarked one day, 'There is a land far away where the men feed the little babies.' Subsequent questionings of anthropologists have so far shed no light at all on this problem, and it seems quite likely that I shall go to the grave in ignorance of what she was really trying to communicate. In any case, why on earth did she want to tell us?

After ladylikeness, the most noticeable thing about Miss Allen was that she was so holy. She was a small woman with sloping shoulders and iron-grey hair loosely fastened into a bun on the nape of her neck, and she wore shapeless dimly-coloured clothes and long strings of dull beads. Her eyes were grey, kind and bright, but even their quality was tempered with this holiness which made you feel a tiny bit uncomfortable. It had certain practical advantages, though. One day, early in my school career, as Miss Allen bent over me, correcting some work I was doing, I glanced up at her, and my attention was caught by the bright nimbus of sunlight shining through the soft down on her upper lip. 'Miss Allen,' I told her, informatively, 'You've got a moustache'. 'Yes, dear, yes', was all she replied, with true Christian forbearance. I suppose that without being able to isolate or analyse it, we suspected that her religion was flawed with sentimentality. She was very apt to refer to Christ (who figured largely in her conversation) as 'Our Lord', 'the Saviour', or worst of all 'Baby Jesu'. Every morning when we arrived at school we had quite a long prayer session, when all twenty or so

33

of us stood in a horseshoe-shape around the old upright piano and alternated mumbled prayers with such hymns as 'There is a green hill far away' which we sang with lugubrious enthusiasm.

We often brought our toys along to school, and one day Redspot broke up the prayer meeting with quite an effective display of independence. Richard was holding him as we stood in our horseshoe; right in the middle of the most sacred bit when we were all supposed to have our heads bowed in silent prayer, he spoke up. 'Ah don't believe in Jesus,' he remarked, conversationally in his own characteristic accent. But Miss Allen was experienced as well as holy. Rising from the piano stool she deftly tweaked the offender from Richard's grasp and set him outside the door, leaning against the staircase wall, for the rest of the morning. Nothing was said until we were putting on our coats to go home for lunch: then 'I don't think you'd better bring Redspot to school any more, dear,' she said. 'I think he's really a little too young just yet.' And that was that.

In spite of the softness of Miss Allen's mien and the squirm-inducing references to Baby Jesu, there must have been a strain of steel in her somewhere, for she instilled in all of us a vein of stoicism that has remained for ever an ideal to be aimed at, even if not always attained. Gillian cannot have been much more than four when she stumbled in getting down from a tram, and grazed her knees quite badly. Our mother, who was with us, advanced with comfort and a clean handkerchief at the ready, but Gillian sternly fended her off. 'No' she said, subduing her trembling lip and winking back the tears that threatened to run down her cheek. 'Don't bother. Miss Allen says that it's good for us to suffer!'

Although I was young to start school, it was made clear to me quite soon that having opted for it, the decision was irreversible. One sunny day I put the matter to the test. It was early June, and down in the rough grass at the side of the front garden the buttercups were just coming out. They were beautiful buttercups. Their leaves were dark green, short-stemmed and succulent, and the flowers were globes of magical brilliance. The outsides of the petals were yellow but downy, like Miss Allen's moustache, and when they first came out that was all you saw. But when they opened under the hot sun you looked right into them and their insides were brilliant like varnish, set off with such a vigorous, sturdy brush of stamens, and centred with the marvellous green glistening pinpoint of the pistil. I had it in mind to spend the afternoon among them, squatting close to the ground on my very short legs and peering face to face at their newly unfurled beauty; so I informed everybody that I wouldn't be going to school any more that day, and took myself off on pleasure bent.

Five minutes later, Gillian arrived, strolling onto the scene with carefully contrived casualness. 'Come on, Libby', she said. 'It's time to get ready for school.' 'I'm not going to school again today,' I told her. But she knew how to manage me. 'If you come along now, without any fuss,' she said, 'when we get home again I'll give you—something *really nice!*' Oh, the innocence of a three-year-old! Of course I jumped up willingly enough and trotted along to school; and equally of course, when I got home at the end of the afternoon and demanded 'something really nice' she expressed herself surprised at my naïveté. 'You really shouldn't have believed me,' she said blandly. I only said that to make you good.' It was my first experience of being manipulated.

So I never tried to stay away from school again, and really I never wanted to. For the bare echoing room, with its tall windows looking out onto the churchyard elms, and its smell of boards, dust and ink, was a magic anteroom through which one passed to fascinating new dimensions of learning. Every new achievement was delightful, for I was still young enough to learn without effort, and I participated with joy in every activity. Sometimes we stitched pictures on cardboard, outlining strange angular chickens and ducklings with yellow wool; sometimes we did 'geography', which consisted of setting out little lead camels and cardboard pyramids in trays of silver sand, while Miss Allen told us about date-palms and oases and black tents made of goat-hair felt; and sometimes we copied out tables in beautiful tall narrow exercise books with blue covers, or chanted them in unison from two times right through to twelve. Reading was no problem. The first book with its big black stories about Nell and Moll and their doll which fell in the rill, was quickly left behind, and before very long we were on Aesop's Fables. It was in this book that I first saw a recognisable picture of God. He was not

35

called God, of course—in fact he was so determinedly plebeian and twentieth-century that I can't think what he was doing in a book of Aesop's fables at all. But there he was, and I knew straight away that he was God; and if I ever do find myself arraigned at the bar on the day of Atonement I shall confidently expect to see him in the judgement seat. He looked extremely nice. He was bald, except for a little fringe of grey hair round the temples and the back of the head, and he wore dark-rimmed spectacles and a striped shirt without a collar, open at the neck. You could only see him down as far as the chest, and he wasn't looking at you either. He was looking down, and he was holding a watering-can with which he was sprinkling water onto something; and whatever it was, he was looking at it with such tender, loving care that one's confidence was immediately engaged. I supposed that he was raining upon the just and the unjust and I liked him a lot better than Baby Jesu straight away.

At playtime we all trooped out into a yard behind the school that was separated only by the width of the ginnel from the end wall of our vegetable garden. But although it was geographically so near to home, the playground was a million miles away in atmosphere, for here we were under the dominion of the big girls, and there was none to help us. Of course they were not as big as all that—the oldest of them cannot have been more than ten—but they exercised their power absolutely, and when they said jump, you jumped, on pain of pinching. What we wanted to do in those playtimes I can't remember—to skip, perhaps, or to bounce a ball against the wall, or simply to 'cronk' down and smell the little border of marigolds that grew down the playground edge, and to feel the wonderful strangeness of their astringent sticky stems between our fingers. But what we had to do instead was always the same. We were divided into two teams—quite arbitrarily, families sundered, brother ripped from sisters as often as not—and then each team was ruthlessly drilled by its general, in preparation for some dreadful combat that nobody wanted to engage in, and that there was never time for anyway. To and fro we marched and wheeled and aligned ourselves, faces set sullenly and boots dragging rebelliously on the pebbles. Over and over again we saluted, while our general, a lanky redheaded maiden possessed of demoniac energy, poured scorn on us with a remarkably wide vocabulary. Uncomfortably we crouched, half hidden beside the buttress, while she unfolded to us her strategy for the defeat of the other side—who, even now, were conspiring unwillingly in the corner by the drinking fountain. The bell for lessons came as a welcome release from these sessions of military dictatorship, but in spite of frustration our leaders persisted with their warlike preparations until they grew too old for Miss Allen's and left.

Back in the schoolroom, peacefully busy, industriously occupied, we soon forgot our troubles. In Miss Allen's presence the tyrants shrank to perfectly manageable dimensions and could even be quite helpful when you missed your way in the blanket-stitch round the edge of your kettle-holder, or forgot to make the long f's in your copy book reach all the way from the top to the bottom lines. 'Stop 'oomin', Libby,' was the worst that one of them ever said to me, and 'Cynthia boomped mah arm', whimpered by a little boy called 'Durrick' was the most serious complaint ever levelled against them.

It cannot have been long after my début at Miss Allen's that a new friend came into our lives, and one who was to be almost like another member of the family. Her name was Marigold, and she was the daughter of the new vicar. 'I want to sit next to Marigold,' I told Miss Allen the first day she appeared in school, and, Miss Allen agreeing, we made friends instantly and with no constraint. She was younger than I was—September to my July—and this tiny edge of seniority was a useful makeweight in future confrontations, for in many ways she could run rings round us, and often did. It was not so much in lessons that she excelled; we were all respectable in that department, with sometimes one and sometimes another getting a nose in front. It was rather in the general ability to cope with the battle of life that she was so much our superior, with a kind of sharpness and insight that none of us could begin to match. In games, for instance, she could beat the three of us; it was always she who devised the first infallible sequence for Chinese checkers, or judged just right in Monopoly whether it was better to have bits of property all round the board or settle for a hotel on Mayfair or Park Lane. Her fingers deftly guided the little silver balls into the eye sockets of clowns in puzzles, or banged the bigger ones into the highest scoring bagatelle enclosures, and in Pelmanism she always managed to remember the card placings, and ended up with the longest string of tricks beside her on the nursery floor.

But in spite of this constant stream of victories, we liked her and she liked us. She was a nice-looking child, rosy and brown, with bright blue eyes and hair of the fairish-brown shade that we always referred to, with unflattering exactitude, as 'dog dirt colour'. Her home was just across the road from ours—the two high garden walls bounded the street for a hundred yards together— and when we were not all at our place, we were all at her's.

One of the delights of the vicarage garden was its apple crop. We had apple trees at home, but as it happened all of ours were cookers, and we wouldn't have been allowed to pick them anyway. But the vicarage apple trees were eaters, Beauty of Bath, and as they ripened early and had no keeping quality, we were at liberty to use them as we liked. There were three trees, close to the grass tennis court, and they leaned their heads together and held down their long sweeping branches in the most obliging way. They were easily climbable too, and it seemed a great expansion of our horizons to perch, six feet off the ground, nibbling the little fragrant fruits at our own sweet will. Up the apple trees was one of our favourite places.

Another was a little hideout that we called the Eagle's Nest. It was really the flat roof of the vicarage downstairs lavatory, which jutted out, obviously an afterthought, from the side of the house. Here the four of us would often foregather, to eat feasts of raw rhubarb sprinkled with sugar and to plan our campaigns against the grown-up world.

Perhaps 'against' is the wrong word, for we were actually very fond of our particular grown-ups, but, banded together in a gang as we were, we felt the need of an opposition, and the forces of grown-updom were often utilised as a kind of lay figure to fill in the blank. Avoiding detection was the chief game, and we would often take it in turns to fetch something from the older house, being on our honour not to be seen in the process, either going or coming.

When were were tired of playing together we would split up

into two pairs, Richard and me together, while Marigold went off with Gillian. I think that the evening-up of our numbers brought about by the advent of Marigold had a lot to do with the relative harmony we all lived in. It may be a sundial-like capacity for monitoring out all but the happy hours that makes me remember so little quarrelling, but I don't think so. I think we really were good friends; and another advantage we had over the squabbling siblings of nowadays was that we were all voracious readers. If one of us should feel grumpy or out of sorts—'having the black dog on your back', Nurse called it—he or she could go off and lose himself in a book for an hour or two, and find distraction from his troubles.

FOUR

BOLAND

There were two big Siberian crab apple trees at East Gate, symmetrically planted at each end of the Little Hill in the front garden. They were exquisite in flower and glorious when the little long-stemmed apples ripened in glistening showers of scarlet and gold. 'Can we 'ave a few o' them cherries, Miss?', a couple of little boys once asked me, and I had to take them to the tree and give them each a rosy fruit to bite before they would believe that the brilliant little things were in fact crab apples, and tasted quite sharp.

We used them for jelly-making, and the rosy-amber, keen-flavoured stuff was something of a *specialité de la maison*. We ate it on bread as well as with lamb or hare; so we got through a lot in the course of a year, and the big brass jam-pan with its arched handle was filled and re-filled several times while the jelly-bags dripped their musical plink, plink in the background.

My first memory of my grandfather shows him up one of these trees, picking the fruit. He is lying at full length along a horizontal bough and reaching out with the handle of a walking-stick for the more distant bunches—and, inexplicably, he is also wearing his canon's hat. This must be a false memory, however, for at that time he was simply a vicar. What one of our daily women pleasingly called his 'canonisation' did not take place until some time later. (A similarlly worthwhile misusage was coined by the receptionist of a skin specialist who used to give patients ultra-violet treatment at his surgery in Leeds. She used to say 'If you will bring your little girl along at 2.30 next Wednesday, Mrs Horner, I will arrange for Dr X to violate her. . .')

For many years our grandfather had been vicar of the parish of Boland, a suburb of Bradford, about five miles from Knearsley.

He and my grandmother were Irish, and both spoke throughout their lives with noticeable Irish accents. Their own children called them Mamma and Papa, but with short a's and the accent on the first syllable, quite unlike the drawling English pronunciation. We called our grandmother Dan-dan, as many children do; but he was always Papa to us as well as to his own children. We slightly altered the pronunciation, however, and said 'Pappar' with the accent evenly divided. He, I am sure, did not mind what anybody called him. He was a most amiable grandfather.

When we were little we saw a good deal of Dan-dan and Papa. Their vicarage was so close that Elspeth would take us over for tea every couple of weeks, and we always enjoyed it. There was only one drawback. Part of the journey lay along a long, straight road called Brick Lane which ran through what would nowadays be described as a trading estate. Small factories surrounded by the paraphernalia of their trades stood around in a wasteland of ashy yards, and at one of them lived a colony of terrible creatures called Woke-wokes. We had never actually seen them, but we knew they were there, and we knew what they looked like too. They were covered in harsh grey fur, and they walked on their hands and feet like mandrils, although they were somewhat bigger. They lived in a fuel tank, a rectangular thing built up about ten feet above the ground, with a metal ladder running up the side of it. They were the very stuff that nightmares are made of, and we always begged Elspeth to go faster, faster, as we sped past their lurking-place.

But we forgot the Woke-wokes as soon as we arrived at Boland. It was a second home to us, although I was never able to love it as my mother did. It was a darker house than ours and colder, and it seemed to me to hide a faint hint of menace or, at least, disapproval. To Elspeth of course it connoted childhood and youth, and all the fun of a large family of brothers and sisters, brewing up gallons of ginger beer and bringing in droves of their friends for long afternoons of tennis on the splendid grass court.

It was a large house, and though in the early 1930's only Arno, my mother's younger sister, still lived with her parents, the others often came to visit. Uncle Percy ('Mac') and Uncle

41

Archey ('Bill') were both out East but one or other of them came home on leave most years, and Auntie Mary, who was married to Uncle Jim, and was the mother of Bruce and Judith, came up from London for several weeks each year.

Bruce and Judith were younger than us, and when Gillian was born Auntie Mary was still unmarried and living at the vicarage. She often used to take her little niece over there for the day, particularly after the birth of Richard, whose arrival Gillian seemed to resent quite a lot. 'I haven't had a single happy day since Ricky was born,' she remarked bitterly at the age of two-and-a-half—which was sad for her, as my father pointed out, for there was less than a year between them, and three hundred and sixty-one days of happiness is a short ration for a whole lifetime, particularly if it's all over before you are even out of your pram.

She was discovered by the verger at the vicarage one sunny Monday afternoon about a year after this outburst, sitting on the front doorstep looking as if all the cares of the world were on her shoulders. 'Where's your A'nty, loov?', he asked her kindly. Gillian looked up at him, her eyes brimming. 'Aunty Mary's gone up for a rest, and Dan-dan's gone out shopping, and I've got to look after this great big house all by myself!', she replied, whereupon she broke down and wept bitterly at her entirely self-inflicted responsibility.

I think that part of the reason that Boland remains in my mind as a house you had to be careful in was that Dan-dan had a sharp way with children. She meant to be kind, I know, and Elspeth always averred that she was leniency itself as a grandmother compared with her performance as a mother, but we all thought she was a bit inclined to jump down your throat. Take the case of the Crinoline Lady for example. It was a birthday present to me, and I admired it very much. It was a pretty little model about four inches tall. The top part was of china, and the crinoline bit was a plump, hard-stuffed cushion of yellow silk. I received it with many expressions of admiration, and then added 'It'll be particularly useful, because I'm just collecting a set of sewing things, and I'll be able to use this for a pincushion.' 'You'll do no such thing!' snapped Dan-dan, very put about. 'You'll put it on your dressing-table and be *very*, *very* careful of it, and if I ever find you so much as putting a pin anywhere near it' et cetera et cetera, with a rousing cadenza on the subject of ingratitude, and children who had so much of everything that they didn't know they were born.

Grandparents now wear the same kind of clothes as anybody else, but in our youth there was a conventional costume for the job so universal that it almost amounted to a uniform. It applied more to the distaff than the spindle side—Papa of course was exempt anyway by virtue of his other uniform of dark grey or black suits and clerical collars—but Dan-dan was a splendidly typical specimen. The well-dressed granny always wore a dress in a limp and drooping material like crepe that came down nearly to her ankles. The basic colour was black, but a pattern of tiny bunches of flowers in bright colours was often scattered all over it. Stockings were of light grey lisle, and shoes were rather like children's bar-fastening house-shoes, except that the toes were more pointed, and they had Louis heels. Spectacles were an obligatory accessory, and they were small and round, with steel frames.

It may seem that I am rather unkind about my poor well-intentioned grandmother, but the fact was that she did take some unconscionable liberties. If she happened to be at East Gate at our bedtime, she would come up to hear us say our prayers—and that in a spirit rather of admonition than of admiration. We resented this. I reckoned to have the praying business nicely worked out at that time; for speed and comprehensive cover, I was sure my prayers had no equal. I included everybody. Yeadon, the gardener, Jessie, the maid, and Ardar, the secretary, had all been added in, and the coda swept up all the odds and ends that I hadn't got around to mentioning individually and tucked them, so to speak, safely into God's care for the night. We were supposed to start with the Lord's prayer, and I went through that reasonably conscientiously, at a walking pace. Then, the formalities being over, I accelerated away and gave God my final instructions at a rattling gallop that got me into bed in about three seconds flat. 'God bless me and take care of me through the night. God bless Mummy and Daddy, Ricky and Gillie, NurseandJessie, YeadonandArdar, andeverysinglegrainofeverysinglething in the world. AMEN.' These words were normally said silently in one's head, with a minimum of embarrassment to

43

everybody. But Dan-dan made us say it all aloud, and if it wasn't to her satisfaction the first time we had to say it again. She also kicked up a trifle at not getting an individual mention in the second part of my prayer, though I pointed out to her that she was safe enough under the all-embracing protection of the last clause. Luckily she did not often visit us in the evening.

Papa was quite different. He liked to indulge us. As soon as we arrived at Boland on one of our afternoon visits, we would run and find him, and the first thing we always wanted to do was go and collect the eggs. For Papa kept hens, white Leghorns (or what passed for white under the all-embracing Bradford soot), which scratched and pecked about under some elderberry bushes in a large but desolate run at the back of the house. The earth was black, and the hens had long worn every vestige of verdure off it; and the prevailing gloom was enhanced by a steep over-hanging artificial bank which loured over the fence where a site had been created for a factory. I remember the look of the bank which was made of red shale, and I remember the smell of the manufacturing process, which was like burning bakelite; but what the firm was, and what were its products I have forgotten. As always, it is the sensory experience that sticks.

The hens were fed on Indian corn, hard, brilliant and beautiful, which was kept in a barrel in the stone-flagged back kitchen. I had forgotten that barrel—or rather I had not thought of it for years—and then when I began to remember Boland, I thought how strange it was that Papa should have had such an enormous store of corn for a flock of about a dozen hens. For in my memory the barrel was vast. It was higher than my head, and so big that I could not have stretched my arms a quarter of the way around it. And then it suddenly struck me that it was not the barrel that was so big, but me who was then so small; the picture in my mind was a genuine flash-back to a view of the world from the angle of a four-year-old.

Papa indulged us further when we stayed to tea. We always had the same food—half a grapefruit followed by a boiled egg, and he would come round to us one after another showing us how to scrape our spoons round the grapefruit to get the last drop of juice. Then, when we were on the egg bit, he would creep round, and with a great display of conspiratorial secrecy,

44

slip a good piece of butter into each of our eggs to melt and blend with the yolk in a symphony of savoury golds.

One unusual and distinctive feature of the vicarage at Boland was the lavatory. It was rather a fine one. It was in the bathroom, but was set in a kind of mahogany stall that reached from floor to ceiling, and its seat was a bench with a hole in it, unlike the conventional horse-collar shape. The crowning glory was the bowl, which was charmingly patterned all over with blue and white flowers. It really was pretty, and if it had survived it would have been worth a lot of money today. It chiefly remains in my mind, though, as the scene of an incident concerning a young man called Horton who was a suitor of my youngest aunt, Arno. He had called in one morning—for coffee, I suppose —and before leaving, he had availed himself of the facilities of the house. The maid was 'doing' the upstairs at the time, and a few minutes after his departure she came into the drawing-room and offered my grandfather a note on a silver salver. 'Mr Horton's just left this in the lavatory, Madam,' she said, her voice and face a picture of mingled puzzlement and outrage. Dan-dan took the note. It was no wonder that the maid thought it odd. It looked like a note because it was printed in handwriting, in bright green ink, but it was actually a little reminder slip that the manufacturers always included near the end of the toilet roll. It read, chattily: 'Your Izal toilet roll is nearly finished. Be sure to get another one'.

FIVE

AUNTIE KATIE'S

When I was very young I had a small and very handsome red Indian doll called Hiawatha, which I adored, and because of him, red Indians and their ways were the first passion of my life. By the time I was three, though, and had started at Miss Allen's, I had changed my totem to horses, which totally preoccupied the remainder of my childhood.

I desperately wanted a pony of my own, but my parents pointed out that this was not possible. 'After all, it isn't only the pony,' they explained. 'You'd need a plot of land to keep it on as well.' This seemed to me not totally beyond the possibility of attainment and when, on one occasion, I had to miss some treat through being too young and was offered anything of my choice as compensation, I instantly suggested 'a pony and a plot of land'. Laughter was, unhappily, the only response to this, and I had to be content instead with a promise of riding lessons in some indeterminate future.

Elspeth was as good as her word, and arranged riding lessons for me when I was six, at an exceedingly up-market riding school about ten miles away from home; I well remember the thrill of scrambling out of the car, all new-jodhpurred, when we arrived for my first lesson. Brushes and wheelbarrows stood propped correctly against the wall; lean, aristocratic heads looked over loose box doors, and a general smell of sweet hay, healthy horses and clean tack filled the air. In one of the stables, through an open door, you could see the row of stalls where the ponies were kept, and on that occasion the first in the line, a tiny bay, was led out for me. James, the gaitered groom, held her head, while The Captain, the owner of the whole magnificent establishment, showed me how to mount and laid the reins correctly in my hands. As we turned away to walk round the school track, I heard him say quietly to James 'Put the saddle on Prince—I'll

46

take her round the home fields if she seems confident enough.'
That was spur enough, if any were needed, and I felt a glow of
pride when, a few minutes later, a tall black was led out, and
The Captain mounted and took me for a proper ride on the
leading rein.

Next week I could hardly wait for the hands of the clock to
creep round to the right time for my next lesson, and sat on the
edge of a chair in the drawing room willing the time along,
clutching a paper bag which contained sugar lumps and carrots
for Minnie. As soon as we arrived at the riding school, I flung
myself out of the car and raced across to the pony stable. But
coming through the door I stopped short and stared in dismay.
Minnie was not there! Instead, in her place was a much slimmer
pony, with no mane and with a neat, short coat of a curious
pinkish-brown. James was in the next stall; he turned round
when he heard me come in, and laughed at my confusion. 'Ay,
it's still Minnie,' he said. 'It's 'er right enough, but she's bin
clipped out since you saw 'er last week. Looks different, doesn't
she? We've 'ogged 'er mane an' all, all tidy for t'winter. But you
a'nt riding Minnie today. Yer've bin promoted. Captain said to
saddle Dolly for you, so 'appen you'd best give t'sugar lumps to
'er instead.'

Dolly was lovely. She was about a hand taller than Minnie—
12.2 maybe—and her colour was a really beautiful dapple grey.
She, too, was clipped out, and her round quarters shone like
dappled apples against the silvery fountain of her long, full tail.
I rode her for about a year, sometimes going out with The
Captain and sometimes with James, and I loved every minute of
it.

A year or so later, Elspeth discovered a riding school much
nearer home—one which we could get to on the bus, and as
Richard and Gillian had started riding now too, we all went
along together. Mr R.'s riding school was an altogether homelier
establishment than The Captain's, with six or seven horses and
ponies stabled in various tarred timber outbuildings dotted about
the home paddock which constituted his school. It was much less
stylish than the other place, but the atmosphere was friendly,
and we liked it straight away.

Mr R. was a small, thin man with spindly legs in incredibly

tight cloth gaiters, and a hard-bitten, hollow-cheeked, hook-nosed face much reddened by the weather. He was much given to fits of silent laughter, and would often pull Star, his lead horse, to a standstill while he indulged in a spasm, doubling over as if in pain and striking his fist repeatedly on his thigh. Straightening up, he would wipe the back of his hand across his eyes to dash away the tears of mirth, and observe mildly 'Ee! Libby! You do mek me smile!' Then, touching his heel to Star's shining flank he would put the cavalcade in motion again until the next time. Perhaps I should admit that it was my naïveté rather than my wit that provoked his outbursts.

Mr R.'s horses were quiet and comfortable, and looked well in spite of the relative shabbiness of their quarters. Only occasionally was there an incident. Once, when I was still on the leading rein, Star decided to 'act up' just as we were turning out of the gate, and reared and plunged very terrifyingly; but Mr R. leaned forward and threw my leading rein to a handy passer-by, and then set about subduing his recalcitrant steed in a truly workmanlike fashion, so that was not very terrible. Another time, a little girl called Ann suddenly began to scream 'Mr R.! Mr R.! I'm going to fall off!' We were only walking at the time, and indeed her mare, feeling her insecure, actually stopped, but off she duly fell in the most determined way. It is the only time I have ever seen anyone fall, with such an air of predestination, from a completely stationary horse. I suppose she must have totally lost her balance.

Another time I managed to get myself dragged, which was not very nice. I was riding a little three-year-old called Betty, and we were galloping along a cindery lane between high hedges of flowering hawthorn. But I had shortened my reins for the gallop, and the long loop of spare that was hanging down got tangled round my foot. I suppose in trying to wriggle it off I must have given the pony a kick because suddenly she bucked, the world swung upside down and I found myself proceeding rapidly up the lane on the back of my head, like Pooh Bear coming downstairs, with one foot caught in the stirrup. Ironically they were a patent safety kind of stirrup, too, which were particularly designed to preclude that kind of accident.

There were no evil consequences from my fall except that I

48

was sick, and had to spend the afternoon in bed with mild concussion, which was unfortunate, as I had one of my school-friends spending the weekend with me.

These wild moments only happened occasionally, of course, and our rides were usually models of tranquillity. As it was a somewhat industrialised district there was perforce a good deal of road work, but it is amazing when you get to know that part of the world how you discover the countryside infiltrating the town, and Mr R. knew all the leafy bridle-paths, the sandy lanes, the fields of friendly farmers and the stretches of common where we could shake our horses up into a canter, so there was no monotony about our rides. Even the road work was not disagreeable in those days. Traffic was trifling compared with what it is now, and we were able to trot along pleasantly, two abreast, in the shade of the sycamores, without getting in anyone's way. There was one favourite place where we always stopped to water the horses when we passed. It was a natural spring that had been channelled into a low drinking trough, and green cressy weeds grew thickly over its bubbling surface. I loved to see the horses' sensitive, whiskery lips, gleaming bits lying slack in their mouths, pushing aside the green weeds to reach the clear water beneath. 'T'weed shows it's clean,' Mr R. always explained. 'They wouldn't drink it, other. Very particular about that sort of thing, is 'osses.'

Mr R. had a little son of about six, called Billy, who rode the horses with diminutive competence. Down at the bottom of the paddock, where the white-painted jumps were, somebody had thrown down an old dandy brush, and Billy insisted that this was a hedgehog. 'Course yer can't see 'is face. 'E's sleeping, 'edge'ogs do, me dad ses so,' he would aver, in the face of all reasonable arguments. One day I made a painting of the riding school for Mr R. and identified for him the spindly, short-necked ponies with which I had peopled it. 'That's Star, and that's Kitty, and that one's Judy—and that's Billy's hedgehog there, down by the jump.' 'Oh aye?' said Mr R. 'Billy's 'edge'og, is it? I thowt it wor a lump of . . . well anyway, loov, it's very tasteful, whatever it is.'

When Hitler's war came, Mr R. was called up, and the riding school had to close down. We also went away to boarding school, an act which gives a totally different tilt to your life. But we didn't miss Mr R. as much as we might have done for it was at this point that we made another acquaintance which was to colour our holiday times for several years. It began with Elspeth.

'I saw some lovely photographs today,' she said one day in the Christmas holidays, 1939. 'You'd have loved them, Libby. It's a patient who lives down at the bottom of Knearsley, and he works as a groom for an old lady in Calveden. She runs a home of rest for old horses, and these photographs are some the *Evening Post* took. I'll take you down next time I call. I'm sure his wife would show you them.'

The patient lived in a fascinating house which opened onto a yard behind a row of shops down at the bottom of the village. A strong, winey smell of pig-swill filled the air of the yard, and from a row of tumbledown buildings on its far side sundry grunts, cluckings, bleatings and stampings bore witness to the presence of a wide selection of animals. A smart little trap, painted black and yellow, stood, shafts tipped skyward, under a tiny Dutch barn, with several trusses of hay, and a fierce-looking Alsatian on a chain barked threateningly at us.

Mrs G., the patient's wife, was proud of the photographs and willingly fetched them out of the drawer to show me. They were lovely. Several ponies in their winter coats, chubby as teddy bears, stood in a thin carpet of snow beside a bare weeping ash tree, solemnly regarding the photographer with large, lustrous eyes. Mr G., the groom, appeared in some of the pictures, leather-gaitered, grinning proudly as he showed off his charges. I praised the ponies to him.

'You oughter get yer Moother to tek you oop to see 'em one day,' he said. 'Miss Millburn'd like to show 'em to you. She don't see many folks, she'd be glad of a visit.' So in due course I met Miss Millburn, and she *was* glad of a visit. We got on so well that she told me to call her 'Auntie Katie', and encouraged us all to come and see her as often as we liked.

She must have been very lonely. I should think she was in her sixties at this time, but as it was still the era when 'old-ladyhood' was a state being embraced by some as early as fifty, it was not possible to be absolutely sure. Her hair was white, certainly, and waved down the sides of her face from a middle parting

rather like the bead curtains that hung across her hall, caught
back to either side. The bead motif was repeated round her neck,
too, where several long strings of them hung, clicking as she
walked rather slowly about. Her shoes were of the authentic
pointed-toed, Louis-heeled strap-fastening granny pattern, and
they were usually made of bronze kid like our dancing pumps.
She was cadaverously thin, and the brown lisle stockings she always wore fell into depressing wrinkles round her shanks for very
lack of anything to support them. Her clothes, which were long,
loose, and shapeless, were of printed crepes, and favoured small
floral patterns of black and orange. But she was not at all gloomy
for all her loneliness, and regarded the world quite skittishly
from behind her solemn tortoiseshell spectacles.

She lived, all alone, in a big stone house which stood at the
end of a long, tree-lined drive, in about sixteen acres of land.
Calveden, like Knearsley, was a curious mixture of urban and
rural, and it too fell victim to the massive pall of soot emitted by
the mills, of which there must have been a hundred or more in
a ten-mile radius. So Auntie Katie's trees had black trunks, and
the warm golden stone of her house and stables had a black
overcast look to it; and if you picked a bunch of the daffodils that
grew so prettily beside the drive, you had to wash your hands
afterwards. Yet the grass grew strong, lavish and green in her
twelve-acre field, and in May the creamy candles weighed down
the horse-chestnuts in its little copses as if they were all in the
depths of the country. A walled garden, with ancient fruit trees
trained against its bricks, separated the main field from the
smaller paddock, and another drive, much shorter, led from the
road into the stable yard.

The house was enormous and, like all under-inhabited places,
singularly cheerless. It was a bigger place than ours, with seven
or eight bedrooms, and one always had the feeling that Auntie
Katie camped in it rather than really living there. She had a cat
called Kitty, a fat, spoilt, neutered tortoiseshell, and I remember
being absolutely 'capped' when I found that this creature had
not only a bedroom of its own, but a bed—a proper human-type
bed, with bedclothes—to which it duly retired each night after
its lavish supper. 'But, after all, why not?' said Auntie Katie,
noticing the surprise on my face at this arrangement. 'She has to

sleep somewhere—and the one thing we're *not* short of in this place is rooms!'

She had been an only child of rich parents—I never heard what was the source of her family's money, but it was usually wool in that area—and, like a good daughter, had stayed at home to care for her parents until they had both died. And so she had found herself, in late middle age, the mistress of a substantial fortune and a typical rich manufacturer's Victorian property, with neither kith nor kin to call her own. Old ladies in this situation commonly lavish their substance on animals, and, being fond of horses, Auntie Katie had elected to turn her place into an equine home of rest, and found with her donkeys and ponies the emotional release that human contacts had evidently never been able to give her.

There were plenty of candidates for a home of rest in those days, when lots of the traffic was pulled by horses, from the massive shires and Clydesdales of the brewers and coal-merchants, through the smart-trotting 'vanners' which pulled the medium loads, down to the small ponies and donkeys belonging to green-grocers, milkmen and rag-and-bone men. Auntie Katie ran her place in conjunction with the R.S.P.C.A., and many a poor old worn-out creature was bought by their inspectors for a pound or two and pensioned off, to spend the evening of its days in happy freedom in the meditative shade of the towering chestnuts.

Not only old ponies came to the home of rest. Some which had been taken from cruel or neglectful masters came to rest and recuperate, before being found good homes where they would be well looked after. Others arrived in very poor condition as a result of illness; some were lame; all were fed and cared for as their needs dictated. In summer they grazed in the big field, and in winter they came back to the paddock, where there was a long low shed that they could go in and out of at will.

If a pony needed stabling properly, there was the old two-stall carriage-horse stable, where low plank gates had been fitted across the ends of the stalls to turn them into loose boxes. The carriage house was used as a hay store, and a lorry-load of hay trusses was delivered every month or so throughout the winter.

The hay itself was ambrosial. It was of a sort you never see nowadays, specially grown for horses, cut from a seeds mixture

52

that had a lot of red clover in it, and grown as a break crop on the big flat arable farms of East Yorkshire. The kind of red clover that farmers used to sow for forage crops was a tall, lanky plant with furry trifoliate leaves and rambling, rather succulent stems. It was difficult to dry properly for hay, but if it was taken just a little bit too green, and 'sweated' in the stack, it developed a sweetness that you couldn't believe if you had never smelled it, and the horses went mad over it. A stack could heat up almost to the point of spontaneous combustion and gradually cool off and cure itself. Then, when it was cut open for the hay to be trussed and sold, its colour inside would have changed to brown, ranging from pale fawn in the cooler areas near the edge to a deep chocolate colour in the middle where the heat had been most intense. These darkest slices were the ponies' favourites and it was comical to watch them nipping and squealing as they struggled for possession of a particularly prized wisp.

There were about six ponies at Miss Millburn's as a rule, and a donkey or two. The donkeys were always called Jenny, regardless of their sex, and being too small to look over the paddock gate, they would look through and beg for tit-bits by making a food-gathering pantomime with their small, soft, mouse-coloured muzzles. Donkeys' eyes are always beautiful under the heavy overhanging thatch of their eyebrows, and they always look wistful no matter how nice a life they are enjoying. The Jennies certainly had nothing to complain about, and succulent carrots, sliced longitudinally to obviate the risk of choking, were passed through the gate to their waving mouths at least twice a day.

The Jennies seemed to be permanent residents, but most of the other ponies came and went. There was Molly, a pretty little black, with slender legs and a tiny well-bred head; she served me a trick once when I went to fetch her up for some reason, and shattered one of my illusions at the same time. I had put the halter on her, and was adjusting it round her ears and her fore-lock, standing directly in front of her, when she suddenly stood right up on her hind legs. Still holding the halter rope, I fell flat on my face in front of her, whereupon she galloped straight over me and high-tailed it to the other end of the field, snorting with self-satisfaction. I had always heard that a horse would never step on a human being, but Molly certainly stepped on me. I had

53

evidence, as T. S. Eliot would say, and no doubt. Her front foot fell full on my buttock, and a circular tear in my shorts was echoed by an even more impressive foot-shaped bruise which I examined with pride that night in the long mirror in my mother's bedroom.

Another of Auntie Katie's ponies was a lovely bright bay called Peter. He was only a youngster, two or three years old, and she did not intend to have him broken in. 'Peter will never know what it is to have a bit in his mouth,' she often used to say, leaning over the wooden post-and-rail fence and looking at him fondly. Alas for Peter! While Mr G. was still there he received a certain amount of discipline, but when that worthy was called up, he was left with no restraint of any kind. Under a regimen of no work, good food, and endless tit-bits, he became in a few months a most poisonous tyrant. He would canter up when anyone went into the field, ears flat back, yellow teeth at the ready, and if carrots were not forthcoming he thought no harm to swing round and bump his rump at you or even lash out with his hind feet. I don't know for sure what happened to Peter in the end, but I suspect he was taken away by one of the close-faced, flat-hatted horsy men who sometimes came to visit Auntie Katie, and subjected to a little wholesome discipline and a touch of hard work. I hope this is what happened to him, because the other alternative for a tiresome pony is dog food, and that would have been a sad end indeed for such a bright young creature.

This somewhat sentimental attitude towards her charges was unfortunately fairly typical of Auntie Katie, and we finally fell out over just such an issue. She had recently acquired a sturdy, dock-tailed dark brown cob called Charles, and as he was broken to both saddle and harness, she said that we could ride him if we wanted to. I had my schoolfriend Gilly (of whose delightful and forceful character I have written in another book) staying with me that holiday, and of course we wanted to take Charlie about a bit and not just moon round and round the field. And a horse that is going to do any amount of road work needs shoes of course, or its feet will be sore. So we took him to the smith in Roddingly and, by pooling our pocket money, got him shod. Auntie Katie nearly hit the roof when we brought him clip-clopping up the drive with his four bright feet all nicely oiled.

You would have thought that we'd sold one of his eyes rather than simply equipping him with a splendid set of new shoes—shoes which, as we pointed out to her, we fully intended to have removed at our own expense at the end of the holidays. She was not amused, and inveighed bitterly against our cheek, opportunism, cruelty to animals and general untrustworthiness in getting him shod without saying anything about it: 'Why you need to go out of the grounds at all I don't know,' she concluded. 'You could have ridden about here. You could have taken it in turns to have rides up and down the drive.' We weren't really on the same wavelength.

Another remark of hers sticks in my mind for sheer breathtaking obviousness. She and I were leaning over the gate one day giving carrots to the ponies, and I was admiring the muzzle of a pony called Pippin. He was a tiny bay, and, as often happens with bays, he had a black muzzle. Not altogether black, but a kind of black picotee which outlined his delicate velvet nostrils and came to a point between them. 'Hasn't Pippin got lovely nostrils?' I said. 'Yes, dear,' replied Auntie Katie. Then she turned to me with the air of one who has an interesting fact to impart, and added 'Did you know, dear, that horses breathe through their nostrils?'

But it would ill become me to be too mocking about Auntie Katie and her funny old-maidish ways and sayings, because she was really very kind to us. I can see her now, shuffling along, toes at ten to two, beaming her sweet and puckish smile behind the white curtains of her hair, hands always outstretched to give something—carrots for us to feed the ponies, glasses of creamy milk and delicious square sponge buns for us, and once a little cut glass vase which she gave me 'to put violets in, dear.' I kept it for years.

It was two miles from our house to hers, and we rode over every morning on our bicycles. The road dipped steeply down to Knearsley Bottom, then rose just as abruptly and unexpectedly turned rural. Up and down it rolled, with green fields on either side, and here and there a spinney of sooty-stemmed sycamores giving a patch of shade. Stone walls bounded the road and divided the fields, and here again the prevailing industrial pall laid its smirch, though not a mill chimney was in sight. It was one of the most characteristic features of that landscape, the way the town and country intermarried. You could have a great big mill with looms and spinning machines and suchlike clattering away hell-for-leather—and then at the back of the mill yard there would be a field, with cows grazing, or rhubarb growing. And so, day by day, we bicycled to Auntie Katie's, and in the rich greenness of her twelve-acre field forgot that we were town-bred.

It ended sadly, however. Soon after the Charlie episode Auntie Katie received word from the powers that be that her twelve acres were to be requisitioned for war production. She was allowed to keep the small paddock and the Jennys, but all the others had to go. Not very long after that, she went herself, with pneumonia. Perhaps she felt that with all her ponies had gone she had nothing particular left to live for.

SIX

SURGERY

In many ways you could say that the surgery was the heart of the house. Certainly its cool smell—with something in it of ether, and something of a freshly-opened tin of elastoplast—penetrated into the hall, and was only gradually annihilated by the other scents of flowers, food, or furniture polish, depending on which door you opened next.

There were three rooms in the surgery. The consulting room was strictly functional, with its scrubbed cork floor, big desk and hard, comfortless examination couch. The waiting room had long padded benches round the walls, and was decorated by a series of large, gloomy prints of Dickens characters. I particularly remember the leering, drunken Bill Sykes, with a dog just like Mrs-next-door's Kish, and Sidney Carton over the fireplace—no doubt in the very act of exclaiming 'It is a far, far better thing . . .' A big roll-top desk in the corner was a never-failing treasury of useful things like paper clips and rubber bands, and in front of it, guarding it from too frequent spoliation by us, sat Ardar.

Ardar (which developed from Gillian's first lisping efforts to say Auntie Dorothy) was our secretary and dispenser, and she had been there so long that it was impossible to imagine the place without her. She was small and plump, with neatly-waved brown hair and cool pale blue eyes that concealed a curious blend of kindly efficiency and a sort of detached worldliness. We children thought she was extravagantly wicked because she averred that she only went to church for the singing—she didn't believe in God at all. We fully expected her to be struck down for this impiety, but the years went by and the Almighty withheld his hand. Her working hours were odd, to fit in with the routine of the practice; but you could have set your watch by her punctuality. Every morning at nine, she arrived; left exactly at twelve;

and came back for afternoon and evening surgeries as required. No situation ever caused her to flap—indeed, I think in the thirty odd years I knew her, I literally never saw her turn a hair, no matter what grisly casualties presented themselves at the surgery door.

The third room of the surgery, and the nicest by far, was the dispensary. Shelves of bottles lined the walls in blue, green, and brown, with long Latin names on their labels, and sometimes the laconic warning POISON in sinister red letters. Bigger bottles—carboys and Winchesters—stood in a group on the floor. A shallow discoloured old porcelain sink, with a high-arched brass mixer-tap, stood under the window, and on the scrubbed wooden workbench that ran along one side of the room were kept the tools of the trade—racks of test-tubes and spirit lamps for testing urine, and pestles, mortars, slabs and palette knives for compounding unguents. Three pointed medicine glass measures in different sizes stood there too, and sometimes when Ardar was particularly cheerful she would pour us each out a tot of our favourite jollop—blackcurrant cough mixture, from one of the big bottles on the floor—and we would quaff it straight from the measure.

We liked to be in the dispensary in the mornings when Ardar was working there. The urine samples would be tested first, and it was interesting to smell the acrid boiling urine gradually overwhelming the clean smell of the little methylated spirit lamp. Then, when the results had been noted, the far-too-generous samples provided by the patients would be swilled down the sink, and the test-tubes cleaned with a special little bottle brush and left to dry upside down on their stand. When we were very little, if we were caught short, Ardar sometimes held us out to urinate into the dispensary sink, to save the trouble of running back into the house. 'After all,' she used to say 'so much urine goes down that sink every day, I'm sure a little more won't make any difference.'

Then Ardar would turn to making up the medicines, from a list that she had prepared from the doctors' lists, and from what they had prescribed at their surgeries. Moving confidently among the ranks of bottles she mixed, diluted, and measured as the case required, funnelling each product into an appropriate bottle,

with the patient's name written on the label. The labels themselves lived in a marvellous piece of furniture at the other end of
the room from the sink. This was a tall chest of many drawers—
higher than my head—of the sort you still see in an old-fashioned
chemist's shop, and it was full of riches. There were some drawers
full of powders, with little scoops to measure them out with.
There were small round liniment bottles, in three sizes; there
were eye-droppers, and pill boxes, ranging from sweet little ones
just right for a robin's egg to big ones that could comfortably
accommodate a cabbage-white caterpillar and a couple of nastur-
tium leaves; there were corks of all sizes, for the medicine bottles,
and finally there were the labels, crisply bundled together,
smelling of gum arabic, and segregated according to whether
they were 'The Mixture', 'The Liniment' or 'The Ointment',
with further fascinating permutations about tea- or tablespoon-
ful, and once, twice, or three times a day.

The medicines were beautiful, like jewels of red, green or
amber in their bottles. One, for cramp, had the fascinating
quality of separating out into two colours of pink, like summer
pudding. But they were never sent out naked. The bottles and
the pill-boxes were all packed in perfect white paper, and sealed
with scarlet sealing-wax, and the faint flavour of the sealing-wax
hung on the air and added its mite to the distinctive, home-like
bouquet of the surgery.

Finally the medicines were arranged in three separate stacks
on the surgery table, and three boys, one from each district, came
to deliver them. Ragged urchins they were, known as 'the
Knearsley boy', 'the Roddingley boy' and 'the Calveden boy',
but to us they seemed god-like, incredibly adult, from their
height of superiority at eleven or twelve years old. We used to
peep at them as they came to collect their clinking burdens for
delivery, but we never dared to address them.

When the surgery was full of patients, of course, we were not
encouraged to enter it. There were times when you had been out
somewhere and, returning found the back door locked, and then
you might have to sidle, smirking fatuously, through the damp,
lugubrious, close-packed ranks; but generally speaking, we had
very little contact with the patients. When we were very young
Thomas occasionally took one of us on his rounds with him,

leaving us sitting in the car with the dog while he went into each house (it is an interesting commentary on the progress of our civilisation that this would be unthinkable now), but this came to an end abruptly when he was surprised in the middle of examining a patient by Richard's piping voice from the bedroom doorway enquiring, 'Daddy, what is that old man lying in bed for?'

When we were a bit older it sometimes fell to our lot to take telephone messages, which we then wrote, with a scratchy dip pen, on the pad on the surgery table. But this could bring its own problems. Thomas, coming in one afternoon, scanned the pad for new calls, and saw that he was required to go immediately to number 27, Wooden Hook. This was quite a puzzle for the poor man for, not surprisingly, there was no street of that name anywhere in the district. The message was clearly written in Gillian's round eight-year-old script, but when he went to look for her to try and gain some illumination she was nowhere to be found. He began to feel quite desperate, for clearly the message was urgent—and then it suddenly occurred to him to say it aloud to himself in a strong Yorkshire accent. That solved it straight away. It was 'Wood Nook'!

Our contacts with the patients being so limited, we did not know many of them, even by sight. Ardar, of course, knew them all, and would greet them as they walked into the surgery, in a friendly way. 'Good evening Mr Brown,' she would say, deftly flicking his card out of the filing cabinet and adding it to the pile on the table. Being Yorkshire, the patients sometimes responded verbally, but as often as not, a slight stiff-necked chuck of the chin, or a murmured 'Na, lass!' was all their reply. Nobody thought anything out of the way, then, when a certain Mr B., in cap, coat and scarf, walked in one winter evening and silently took his place on the waiting seats after pausing briefly by the table to be recognised. He waited patiently for about twenty minutes until it was his turn, then entered the consulting room, and stood mutely by the desk. My mother was sitting there, writing her comments on the last case, and she told us about it years later. 'I went on writing for a minute or so, and he just stood there. And then I finished, and said to him "Now then, Mr B., what can I do for you?" And he fixed me with a gloomy

60

stare, still not saying anything, and slowly began to unwind the scarf from his neck. And then he tipped his head back, and suddenly I was looking right down into his lungs! He'd been trying to commit suicide by cutting his throat with a breadknife, and all he'd managed to do was to saw halfway through his trachea! And then he suddenly decided it wasn't such a good idea after all, and came along to the surgery to get himself stitched up! But just imagine him walking in and just sitting there all that time patiently waiting his turn!'

Some of Thomas's more bizarre experiences came through his job as police surgeon. Usually this meant doing post mortems, but on one occasion at least it got a bit more exciting. A posse of policemen arrived hammering on the door one wet and windy night, and called him out to deal with what they described as 'an urgent medical problem'. It appeared that a certain man in the village, well known for his violent and destructive passions, had drunk himself into a frenzy, and had then, after terrorising his wife and children, rushed upstairs and locked himself into a bedroom with a carving knife with which, he loudly and repeatedly declared, he would slit up the first person to cross the threshold. After which, he would 'do himself in'. 'And as it seemed a psychological sort of case, like,' explained the sergeant shamelessly, 'we thowt it would be more oop your street, Doctor. If you know what Ah mean.'

Thomas knew what he meant all right. But short of acknowledging himself afraid, there didn't seem to be much he could do except get in there and hope for the best. Outside the bedroom door, he marshalled his forces. Two of the biggest policemen were chosen to help him charge down the door; he hoped that in the confusion of their entry, he might be able to seize the man's wrist and disarm him, or at least bring him to the floor with a kind of Rugby tackle.

The three of them took their places. A sinister silence had succeeded the volleys of oaths and threats from the bedroom. Whatever was going on in there? Was the man crouched, waiting, just inside, with hand raised, ready to strike? Or had he, in a drunken despair, plunged the knife into his own body? There was no way to find out but by breaking down the door. Thomas nodded, and as the three of them lunged forward, it gave with a

61

splintering crash. Thomas, being foremost, half fell into the room.

And then the big drama collapsed into a scene of the utmost bathos. There lay the knife on the floor, and away on the other side of the bed knelt the man, saying his prayers. Maudlin tears of self-reproach coursed down his cheeks as he brokenly besought the Almighty's forgiveness for his manifold sins and wickedness.

Thomas dusted some splinters off the shoulder of his jacket, and picking up the carving knife handed it to the sergeant. 'I think that should solve your urgent medical problem, Sergeant,' he remarked, 'so if you'll excuse me, I'll be on my way.' The sergeant had the grace to avoid his eye.

The letters were delivered at East Gate early enough to appear at the breakfast table, and there were often extracts funny enough to be read out—not, of course, including anything confidential! We had one patient who was a great correspondent—an authoress *manquée*, Elspeth used to say—who wrote two or three letters a week, many-paged, in a laborious violet scrawl on cheap, lined paper. Since they were mainly detailed accounts of her 'symptomons' they were not passed round, but she had one delightful literary habit which we all enjoyed, of sprinkling her missives with foreign phrases, obviously culled from a list in the back of a dictionary. 'I non mi ricordo whether I mentioned to you on your visit last thursday, doctor . . .' she would write airily, or 'I should be glad if you would send me a prescription pour encourager les autres.' As she was a woman of absolutely no education, the adornments were sprinkled rather arbitrarily about the letters, but the total effect was quite engaging. Another of her little ways was to continue the description of her 'symptomons' all down the back of the envelope if she didn't feel the tail end of her letter warranted another page. Then the postman was able to enjoy them as well as the doctor.

Another letter from a patient so took my fancy that, after it had been answered, I kept it for some time, and accidentally committed it to memory. I know it still:

Dear Sir Doctor,
    Because I am very nervous and I had by my work—as a weaver

—dizz-iness, so that I not know what I did at this moment, I must my work expressed.

I should like a quiet work, and I request, Sir, that you will be so kindly and will give me a not for Labour Exchange, that the change my work is necessary for recover mine health.

I will be very thankful to Sir for it,

Yours faithfully,

P.S. I have also a sultriness in breast and press under right shoulder; on left ear I heard very little and mine eyes are very weak.

P.S. As a Pole (ex-soldier in the last war) I have still many trouble with English language but I hope, that you will this understand.

I think he achieved a triumph of self-expression; what a happy chance that the dictionary should lead him to a word like 'sultriness'! 'A sultriness in breast'! I know exactly what he meant straight away. And the rhythm has—surely, again, by chance—something of the plaintive cadence of the psalms.

The best letter was written by an old man to the Minister of Health, complaining about virtually every member of our practice, but never posted. When, in the natural course of events, he died aged about seventy-nine, the letter was found among his effects and passed to my father, and it became a stock source of quotations for all the family. It was long and rambling, giving details of various alleged mis-treatments et cetera by virtually every doctor in the district, and attributing spendidly improbable speeches to everybody. He had some leg ailment for which he was being treated, and some bottle or other of medicine that had been prescribed for him had, he averred, given him 'a burning feeling'. He describes how he had mentioned this to one Dr B. in our firm, 'At which he turned away and replied "If that's so, take the lot, Sahib!" I learned afterwards that he had been in India, Burma.' Then my father went to see him and looked at his leg 'Whereupon he said all well and good but what was all the blue?' Another thing Thomas was supposed to have said was 'There as been a slip-up.' There was a lot more very quotable stuff, but unfortunately the original got mislaid.

The best letters for quoting that ever came into the family, though, were not from a patient but from a suitor of one of my aunts; and even making allowance for the fact that they were penned sixty years ago, it is hard to conceive that they were not intended as pastiches. Those who knew the young man, however, assure us that they would have been written in dead earnest. He was a poet—a Poet, rather (let us give him his due), and apparently a prolific one. He writes 'Here is a sonnet—one of half a dozen that I threw off before breakfast this morning. Methinks it hath something of sonority and power.' On another occasion he protests the depth of his love: 'Should but your dainty handkerchief fall into a whirlpool, I would dive after it—to death if need be!'

But his best effort was after he had got as far as proposing, when he was urging his suit. 'What of means?, some more mercenarily-minded persons may ask. Give me but the daily inspiration of your presence, and I will pour forth such a flood of literature of high market value as to settle all doubts on that score!' I simply love 'high market value'.

Needless to say, he was rejected, and passed out of the family's ken. I have never seen any of his sonorous and powerful works published in any anthology; but at least some of his writing has attained a small, local immortality.

Another piece of gnomic wisdom that we always remembered came in a letter written to one of the maids by her suitor, Percy Dobson. The course of Percy's true love had been sent awry by some unfounded malicious gossip, and his sweet-heart wrote that he had deceived her, and that she never wanted to see him again. In his reply he repudiated the charges, and finished with a phrase which became a family proverb: 'If everybody minding they own binnus they plenty on.' It sounds as if it could have come from the mouth of Uncle Remus.

A man who acted as caretaker for one of our outlying surgeries was a good source of mispronunciations and malapropisms. Describing an unfortunate fire which had gutted his henshed and killed all his hens, he said 'Ah went to oppen t'door, to try to get 'em out, but it wor 'opeless. It were like a furno in there—a ragin' furno!' He had his own words, too, to describe the start of the blaze. 'It wor t'stove—it must've exploded. I kept it in

64

there when t'weather were cold. It were one of them velour stoves, yer knaw . . .'

To some extent these people deserved to be quoted in that they genuinely were the authors of the remarks attributed to them. Others were not so lucky. One doctor that we all knew—Dr Bloggins, I will call him, though that was not his name—collected a whole battery of observations that were made not by him but by a doctor in a film we all saw. There was a decided resemblance between them. They both had exactly the same way of tucking their chins into their necks and smiling with their mouths on one side, and there was a similarity, too, in the somewhat bland, not so say patronising way in which they responded to criticism. 'I think you're a contemptible doctor!' 'You won't when you see the size of my bill,' we would say to each other, after we had seen the film, imitating as best we could the rather fatherly, pedestrian, sub-Yorkshire accent of Dr B. The simple phrase 'I know' said by the doctor in the film formed the basis for our most fruitful flights of fancy. The game—since played in the *Sunday Times*—was to devise as many questions as possible that would elicit something reasonably similar to these sounds, always allowing for the Yorkshire accent. Thus: Q. What is the principal export of Sweden, Dr Bloggins? A. Iron ore. Q. What are the other vowels leaving aside E, A and U, Dr Bloggins? A. I an' O. Q. If you were an itinerant vendor of radioactive fuels, Dr B., what would be your street cry? A. 'Ion-oh!' and so on. Some of the questions got very complex indeed. Q. What number would you place in what relation to two to make a half, Dr B.? Answer in German and Scottish, please! A. Ein o'er. Another fantasy that grew from this game was Dr Bloggins' alleged invention of a mechanical prostitute, called the Iron Whore, which anticipated the lifesize collapsible bedmate of the sixties by two decades. In the myth it spent most of its time on the test bed, however, and never really saw the light of day as a commercial proposition.

When you telephoned Dr Bloggins, he replied, naturally enough, 'Dr Bloggins speaking' as he picked up the receiver. This was transmuted into another game where you had to indicate by subtle actions or intonations what else he might be doing that rhymed—Dr Bloggins shrieking, Dr Bloggins peeking,

65

Dr Bloggins squeaking, or creaking, or leaking—for example. When we had exhausted most of the possibilities, we did enlarge the rules to admit assonance and were thus able to include Dr Bloggins cheating, bleeping, leaping, creeping, excreting, and so on. It was a game that needed no introduction. Anyone who spoke in that particular voice, with one shoulder hunched and his mouth pulled round to one side was Dr Bloggins, and the developments happened quite naturally. I trust he never knew how extremely we took his name in vain. He was a nice man, really, and didn't really deserve to be such a universal figure of fun.

Other imitable doctors were some of the locums who came to work for a month or so while Thomas and Elspeth went away on holiday. Dr W. was one of these, an Irishman, with a brogue so thick and a delivery so rapid and sotto voce that it was a real job to know what he was saying. His best effort concerned Ardar. A busy evening surgery was in progress and she was working in the dispensary. Suddenly the door opened and Dr W. came in, propelling a man before him. 'Will you syringe this man's ear out, please?' he said—she thought—and disappeared. Ardar often did little jobs like ear-syringeing, being a thoroughly experienced doctor's aide. 'Which side?' she asked the man, and he replied 'Me left.' 'Sit down there, please,' she told him, pushing forward the dispensary chair, and he obediently sat, while she busied herself getting everything ready. She mixed up the jugful of warm soapy water and got out the syringe, then hung a towel round his neck, while he stared at her with increasing alarm and puzzlement. Then, having filled her syringe, she advanced confidently upon him, but he wriggled out from her grasp and rushed to the other side of the room where he assumed a defensive posture, crying out 'There's nowt wrong wi' me ears, tha knaws! Ah've twisted me knee, that's all!' Ardar referred back to Dr W. 'What did you say about that man you just sent in to me?' she asked. Dr W. looked up, surprised. 'I said "Ung. Meth. Sal." ' he said, giving the abbreviated form of the name of an ointment more popularly known as wintergreen ... Since this incident we have tried and tried, using every inflection of the human voice and every possible variation of an Irish accent, to make 'Ung. Meth. Sal.' sound like 'Will you syringe this man's ear out please?' but with a signal lack of success.

As for the man, he was calmed and pacified and sent off with his box of ointment, but we often imagined him telling his wife about the incident. 'Ee! They aren't 'arf thorough oop at t'doctor's! Ah went in wi' me leg and they near as dammit gave me ears a good wash out at t'same time!'

SEVEN

GRANDMA

When we were young children one of the events we most looked forward to was a visit from Thomas's mother, who was known to us as 'Grandma' or sometimes 'Grandma Armitage'. She had a different name from us because she had been married twice. Her first husband, the father of her two children, was sixty-five when they married; she was twenty-three. And after his death, twenty-one years later, and several years of widowhood, when she married for the second time she once more chose a man substantially older than herself. So presumably that must have been how she liked them.

Looking back from a generation which has grown accustomed to lightning psycho-analysis I sometimes wonder if perhaps she suffered—if that is the right word—from a touch of father-fixation. For her own father was an extremely dominating man, and his tiny wife (only four foot ten inches in her stocking feet), and many children adored him with an almost religious fanaticism, particularly the girls. For my money he sounded a most tiresome and self-admiring old fool, but there is no denying that the climate of opinion has changed, and presumably in the period (circa 1860–1880) when he flourished, the sort of chauvinistic strutting that he indulged in was much admired. 'I shall be leaving for church in precisely seven minutes from now,' he used to say. 'If my dear wife is ready to accompany me, I shall be happy to escort her. If not, I shall go alone.' An even less endearing habit of his was to dominate both lunch and supper on a Sunday by repeating the morning and evening sermons, respectively, almost word for word. But instead of pelting him with the flat silver and stuffing the table cloth in his silly prating mouth, which is what he surely deserved, his daughters sat round all eagerly attentive, and boasted to everyone they knew about their Papa's strong character and prodigious feats of memory.

Perhaps it was from him that the gene for a good memory came, for that was certainly one of the qualities that his two grandchildren showed, together with a persistent intellectual curiosity, a brilliant, if wayward, creativity and an independence of judgement that took nothing for granted, not even the god-like nature of a grandfather. He was dead, as it happened, before little Tom and Phyllis were born, so no actual clash of personalities ever took place, but Thomas could not slip into the family attitude of reverence as easily as his aunts seemed to expect him to. 'Oh Tom!' they used to say to him, 'It's such a loss to you that you never knew your grandfather! If only he'd been alive, he'd have taken you down to the railway station to show you the trains, and he'd have said to you "Look at those great big wheels..."' 'And I used to think to myself, even when I was only four or so', said Thomas, 'silly old fool, as if I couldn't see for myself that they're great big wheels without having to have it pointed out to me...'

Grandma was one of those women, fortunate perhaps, who seem to grow better-looking as they get older. She was quite a pretty girl—indeed, the whole family were handsome, and the females were known in their own locality as 'the nine beautiful Colby sisters'—but judging by photographs, her face gained in distinction as she got older and by early middle age she was really beautiful. She had a lovely nose for one thing—a perfect, exquisite, chiselled little nose whose immaculate shape was also inherited by her daughter; and she had lovely eyes, hazel with dark lashes, which glowed with life, fun and gentleness.

It is a lucky thing for the men in her life when a woman is born with a gentle nature. And Grandma seemed absolutely cut out for the traditional woman's role in society, a position that she filled with grace and satisfaction during the whole of her life.

She was immensely domestic. Her house was her kingdom, and if she was given the monarch's divine right therein she had no further territorial ambitions. She was a wonderful cook, a notable housekeeper, and a great trainer of maids. She knew how everything should be done, and allowed no short-cuts in the domestic rituals, so that a house spring-cleaned by her—or under her supervision—really was 'bottomed' in the true Yorkshire tradition. Thoroughness was a religion with her and as a good priest

69

should, she saw to it that every acolyte was punctilious in its observances. So come spring-cleaning time everything was disturbed. Every carpet was hung on the line and beaten in the wind to shake free the grit of the winter's traffic; every drawer was emptied and re-lined with paper, and every inch of paint-work washed down. Fresh distemper was slapped on where it was appropriate and all the curtains and chair-covers were washed. This spring-cleaning bug never left her, for in the war, when she was well over seventy and living at East Gate I remember a letter from Elspeth which began 'Today is bright and sunny, with a brisk north-west wind blowing; and as soon as Grandma woke up this morning and saw what kind of day it was, she leapt out of bed and washed all her blankets, which are now flapping magnificently on the clothes-line in the yard.'

Grandma was not an intellectual, and as both her children were, they used to tease her gently, which she rather liked. 'Ee Tom!' she would protest, deprecatingly, at some of his flights of fancy (she had a touch of Yorkshire accent and often said 'Ee!'), but she couldn't help laughing though I never heard her say anything intentionally improper herself. She was not safe from her lively children however; they were ever on the *qui vive* for absurdities and if they weren't there already they would invent them. Thus, as Grandma had a habit of referring to her first husband always as 'Tom's father', they endowed the dear old family doctor, who often came to see her, with the title 'Phyllis's father' which always made her giggle, even while she was saying reprovingly 'Ee! Tom! Phyllis! You really mustn't say things like that!'

Another time she really laid it in their laps when she was unlucky enough on the bus to have the vacant seat beside her taken by a musician with a 'cello or something in a case which much incommoded her when she rose to get off at her stop. 'He *was* a nasty man!' (she was always being persecuted by nasty men which, being Yorkshire, she pronounced of course năsty). 'There he was, right in the way, and he wouldn't move when I wanted to get out. So I'm afraid I kicked his instrument. Well, it was his own fault . . .' Thomas eventually enshrined this in an operetta in which Grandma sings a song on her favourite topic:

The nǎsty men, the nǎsty men, they're always after me,
They chase me down the stairs, they catch me unawares.
One nǎsty brute, all black with soot, was in the oven—then,
Last night when I got into bed
A nǎsty man was there, who said
'Please don't get up for me—I'm dead!'
The nǎsty, nǎsty men.

I don't remember all of it, but the musician incident ran:

And then he has me in a fix
When out his instrument he sticks;
It's hard to kick against the pricks
Of nǎsty, nǎsty men.

Grandma was always fond of antiques, and several of the nicest
things I have were originally acquired by her. Curiously enough
I find in myself particularly well-developed the two tastes in
which she was most acquisitive. Like her, I can't stop buying
china, and like her, I often buy material because I like it, and
then just keep it in a drawer for years without using it. After
her death, various bolts of chintz were discovered among her
effects, put by for some eventuality which never happened; and
her china, packed into tea-chests during the war, filled a whole
room of our cellar, and formed the basis for a recurring dream
which I still have from time to time. I dream that in some
unspecified way, I have become the owner of a house with all its
contents, and in the dream I am going in for the first time to
have a look at my new property. In the kitchen are several deep
china-cupboards, stacked to the brim with stuff, and I open them
and look in. What is in front is useful but not very decorative—
pudding-basins, perhaps, and stacks of white dinner plates. But
the cupboards are very deep, and as I peer in, my eye is caught
by a glimpse of colour in the shadows behind. I move the plates,
and there is a little treasure—a Rockingham jug, perhaps, a little
rococo frisking of green, white and gold. And behind it again,
what is that? A Chelsea tureen, in the form of a cabbage—a
couple of Bow figures—a Worcester bowl—and so on and so
forth until my subconscious has had its fill of unreality and I
wake up. I usually get a good run for my money first, though,

71

and look into cupboard after cupboard until I am reeling with the richness of it all; and a sense of good fortune usually stays with me after this dream for the whole of the following day.

Grandma was an indefatigable shopper who could run three ordinary women off their feet and still come home at a hand canter; and as well as going round the conventional shops of Leeds, she liked to attend auctions. Fortunately for her, she did not have to go alone. One of her sisters, Auntie Flo, had married a man called Edgar, who had an antique shop in Pickering, so the two sisters often went buying together, increasing their knowledge of the antique business as they went along.

Auntie Flo was a curious woman in some ways. When my Aunt Phyllis got engaged to Uncle George she wanted to introduce him to her relations, so together they paid a visit to Flo and Edgar at the shop in Pickering. After the courtesies had been exchanged, Auntie Flo said 'I've been meaning to send you a wedding present, but since you're here, perhaps you'd like to choose one for yourselves. Look around the shop, and see if there's anything you'd like.' So George and Phyllis looked and finally settled, modestly enough, on a little three-legged pine table. They pointed it out to her as their choice, and she glanced at it across the shop. 'Oh, you like the little cricket table, do you?' she said. 'All right—you can have that then—for thirty shillings!' An odd way of giving a present. But they still have the table.

I only met Auntie Flo once, when she must have been in her late seventies or early eighties, the Colbys all being a long-lived lot. She was still in the antique shop in Pickering with Uncle Edgar, who remains in my mind as little, bent, and rosy, with a shock of silky white hair, exactly like one of those little men who come out of Austrian barometers when the weather is going to be fine—or is it wet? She gave us presents on that occasion which we all still have, and as far as I am aware she didn't charge for them. She gave Gillian a little china pig with clover flowers painted on his back; and Richard a little pair of sitting-up dogs in red and white; and me a china pot for the dressing-table, on whose lid was a beautiful brightly-coloured swan, with two cygnets.

Although Grandma came to see us two or three times a year,

her main home, after Pa's death, was with Phyllis and George. She and Phyllis shared a love of beautiful things and treated with reverence the lovely pieces of antique furniture that she had brought with her, but for some reason she cherished the most unjustified suspicions of George, and quite unnecessarily guarded her beloved possessions from him as a mother tiger might have guarded her young. The thing is, he was a Man and Man, in Grandma's book, was the great Incalculable, against whom Woman was wise to forearm herself in every way possible, and most of all in the protection of that which was most dear to her and nearest to her heart—to wit, her furniture.

There was the sofa, for instance. It was very precious. Grandma bought it in a sale, had it delivered home and hung around it like a lover calling all to see and to comment on its beauty, its uniqueness, and its supreme fitness for its purpose. It was rather nice. It was a two-seater, covered all over in gros point, in a design of chevrons, and it must be acknowledged that it arrived at the house in absolutely mint condition. And Grandma determined it should stay so. So she made it a cover. After all, she reasoned, if she left it in a state of nature, George might sit on it. And if he did, he would find it so comfortable that he would probably take to sitting on it every night. And if he did *that* no doubt he would always sit on exactly the same place and would eventually wear out part of the needlework with his great crude awkward male bottom, and her lovely sofa would be spoiled. So a cover it must have, and a cover it duly got.

It was such a pretty cover. It was glazed chintz, with little bunches of roses scattered all over it and a little frill which demurely covered the sofa's legs and hung down to the ground. It looked really charming; so pretty in fact that it made the sofa look really inviting, and roused fresh doubt in Grandma's mind. After all, George might *sit* on it . . . So she had another cover made to go over the top of the first cover, in brown holland this time, and in order that George should not still feel tempted to sit on it and, who knows?, possibly break its springs, she moved it into the dining room. And there it stood, all covered up. And nobody sat on it or noticed it or ever even got a glimpse of the lovely needlework that had first caught her eye and made her buy it, right up to the day of her death.

But after her death it was brought forth, and stripped to the buff, or rather, to the gros-point, and George *did* sit on it for many years, and such was the quality of the needlework that his great big male bottom made no impression on it whatsoever and that sofa is in as mint a condition today as it was when Grandma bought it all those years ago.

Grandma, as I have said, was a notable cook and a great house-keeper; but however her descendants may remember and admire her standards there is no way in which we can emulate them. For to live today on the sort of food that Grandma took for granted, you would have to be a millionaire. She was, I suppose, middle-class—comfortably off, certainly, but not rich. Her father was a colliery manager, her first husband owned a printing and en-graving business, her second husband owned a string of quarries; but whenever she went out to shop for anything from bed linen to beef, from polish to potatoes, there was only one quality—the best. And she was not alone in this. As far as I can gather, the middle classes of her day lived with a lavishness that is absolutely inconceivable to us now, demanding not only an unvaryingly high standard of quality in the goods they bought, but an enormous quantity of things as well. Some years ago, by chance we discovered, in an old apothecary's pot that stood on the drawing-room mantelpiece, a couple of Grandma's grocery bills, dating from 1912. They were an absolute revelation. Luckily they were fully itemised and priced out, and luckily too they were for successive weeks, so that they must have been fairly ordinary orders, not special stockings-up; and how in the world a normal household managed to get through that kind of food in a week beggars comprehension. The enormous quantity of flour draws attention to the fact that all the bread and cakes were home-made, and also to the fact that to be a good bread-eater was accounted unto you for a virtue in those days. Presumably eating a lot of bread indicated that you weren't 'fancy' and picky about your food—though no cake, however tarted up, could possibly be more delicious than those big, springy, close-textured loaves of new bread, not to mention the wonderful tea-cakes and long-buns, spicy with peel, that were always made at the same time. It is no wonder that people tended to a touch of embonpoint in those days, though the Yorkshire word 'bonny'

74

which described such a figure made it sound rather nice. The young, of course, who ate with no thought of the morrow, were encouraged to out-do even their parents' brisk performances as trenchermen; and when Thomas was in the sixth form at Leeds Grammar School, in the summer he habitually bowled, fast, for an hour in the nets after school, and then walked home and ate a whole large loaf of the home-made bread and a pot of strawberry jam for his tea.

I don't know whether Grandma did most of the cooking in her own home or whether she only made certain special things and left the rest to the maid. But some things she was famous for, and those she would always have been solely responsible for. Like her rabbit pie, for instance—though it was 'rabbit', really, only by courtesy, for the recipe called for at least as much prime beef and succulent gammon as rabbit, all cooked in a rich gravy beneath its crisp, brown, wafery, high-puffed crust.

When Grandma came to live with us at the beginning of the war, we had no living-in maids, and she did quite a bit of the cooking. She had one little special knife that she was very fond of, and nobody else was supposed to use it. It was called 'The Old Hundredth', and it was a small vegetable knife with a notched and yellow bone handle, and a wicked little real steel blade, half worn away with much sharpening. A flight of seven or eight stone steps led from the back door down to the yard, and it was on the top one of these that Grandma whetted her weapon. In time she wore quite a groove in the stone, which I dare say is still there, though Grandma and the Old Hundredth have gone their separate ways many years ago now. It is in the kitchen that I remember her best, standing by the table with the Old Hundredth in her hand, and smiling at me, with her bright, loving eyes, as she tells me how clever I am to be able to use a potato peeler. 'I could never master one of those, love.' And though I am nine, and I know that I jolly well *ought* to be able to use a potato peeler, I still feel warmed by her approval, and inspired to peel the potatoes faster and faster. 'It takes off a lovely thin peel, much thinner than my Old Hundredth,' she says, examining one of the narrow ribbons of potato-skin curling into the bowl of water. 'But of course that doesn't matter as much as it did, now we've got the thi Hens.'

For, with the war having just started, we had embarked on this new, exciting branch of livestock husbandry, and Grandma, as chief Henwife, always dignified them with a verbal capital letter and with a special, more reverential pronunciation of the definite article which made it more like a 'thi' than an ordinary, everyday, common-or-garden 'the'.

When we first decided, in the interests of greater self-sufficiency, to become a family of hen-keepers we had to find a suitable place for their accommodation; but this was no great problem. When the house was built in the early 1860s the amenities included a useful stable block, with a carriage house and tack room, stalls for two, and single loose box, with a couple of big lofts over the whole lot for a forage store, and the groom's bedroom. The most obvious bit for hen-house conversion was the loose box, for the coach house was now my father's garage, and my mother's car resided in the stall area—with the stall partition removed, of course. You could still see on the walls the graceful sweep of the boarding that had once protected the carriage horses, and the hay racks too, high in the corners, bore mute testimony to the glory that was departed. I often used to hang around in there when the car was out, and try to imagine it as it must have been in its heyday—the bustle of activity in the mornings, with the groom in his shirt-sleeves strapping one of the horses out in the yard—you could see the ring on the wall where the horse was tied up—while the boy ran hither and thither with forkfuls of hay and sieves of oats, and the 'odd man' squeezed out his chamois leather to give a last, loving polish to the shiny black and yellow dog-cart. But the cars had to be housed, and the glamour was gone; the dog slept in the tack room, junk gradually filled the lofts, and the loose box was only used for the storage of garden tools, which could perfectly well be accommodated elsewhere—for example, in with the dog.

So the tools were cleared out, the fine, square, bluish tiles of the floor were brushed clean, and several converted orange boxes were lined with straw and put round the walls for laying in. A long perch was installed across the full width of the box, with a wide droppings board beneath it. Wooden feed troughs and a heavy glazed drinking bowl were provided, and then we were ready for our first hen delivery.

76

They were a motley lot, the first hens. They were provided for us by Rawland the fishmonger, who had a little farm as well as his shop; and in addition to the birds themselves, he sold us tail-corn (which is the small corn separated out by the threshing-machine as too thin to be worth milling) and potatoes, which formed the bulk of their feed. And he gave us good advice. Papa gave us advice too, and we also bought booklets issued by the Food Office, and one way and another we managed very well.

Grandma, as it happened, was not totally inexperienced with poultry, having had them in her early married life when she lived in the country, but wartime shortages of foodstuffs meant that a different system had to be devised, and it did entail a lot more work than just scattering a few handfuls of Indian corn.

If you decided to keep hens during the period of food rationing, you forfeited your egg coupons and received instead coupons which entitled you to a certain amount of hen-food. The number of hens you managed to keep on this ration was entirely up to you, and if money was not too much of a problem there were plenty of ways of augmenting the ration, as we very soon discovered. It also helped to have other people registered with you, for they gave you their coupons and you drew the extra meal and kept a few more hens; and it helped them too, for there was no difficulty in giving them four or five times as many eggs as they would have got from a grocer, and the freshness and quality could always be guaranteed.

Our hens had a pleasant life. They were let out of their loose box in the morning as soon as the household was stirring, into one of two alternative ranges. One was approached by a pop-hole in the back wall of the loose box, where a stone had been removed, and that led them into the vegetable garden. A large section had been wired off for them, with a fair grass plot, and a deep surrounding fringe of young sycamores and elderberry bushes under which they skulked when the weather was hot, and hollowed out dust-baths in which they 'bathered'. The other range, which was opened out to them when they had worn all the grass off the first, was more extensive. The pop-hole would be re-stoppered with its stone and the loose box door opened instead so that they could come out into the yard and walk down some shallow steps into the little orchard where the apples,

77

blackcurrants, raspberries and gooseberries grew, which was called the Side Garden.

The morning feed was the main meal of the day and this was prepared for them by their curator as soon as we had finished our own breakfast. A particular old-fashioned black cast-iron pan was dedicated to their use and this was filled with special chat potatoes (small ones) which were boiled up, with the previous evening's peelings, until all was soft and done. The potatoes, strained, were transferred to an enamel washing-up bowl and carried to the boot-cleaning, cat-kittening, dog-biscuit-storing room called the Long Kitchen, from whence their strong earthy smell fought hard to get into every corner of the house. Then they were bashed with a special instrument which sliced them up with strained wires and reduced them to pulp in a remarkably short space of time. Then various things were added to the mash. Sometimes there were lights, horrid loathsome glutinous lumps with all-too-recognisable bronchial tubes dangling out of them which one fished, gipping, out of the pan and minced, rapidly, with averted eyes. Then there was the balancer meal, a mixture of ground barley and fishmeal whose nice sane healthy smell made the business seem quite wholesome again; and finally we would add a carefully measured quantity of Karswood poultry spice, a fragrant paprika-like substance in which could be discerned the wing-shards of ground-up insects, and which imparted quite an exotic savour to the steaming bowlful.

The food was served to the hens in wooden troughs, and dispatched in a very few minutes. Then their water bowl was scoured out and refilled and their grit supply checked. They had to have two kinds of grit freely available to them—limestone grit or oyster shell, to help in the formation of their eggs, and flint grit which they kept in their gizzards to grind up their food; for hens, of course, are like all other birds in that they have no teeth, and the chewing is done further down the alimentary tract.

The hens' second feed was a measure of corn, which was scattered in the loose box on the thick bed of dry peat moss that formed their litter. Here they scratched and pecked about, and when the natural daylight began to fade they were closed in for the night. But in winter their period of activity was prolonged by having a light bulb in their house which was switched off

78

only when we went to bed at half past ten or eleven. It is surprising how few people among domestic hen-keepers know about the difference that this simple aid can make to the number of eggs a hen can lay. Our hens laid just as well in the winter as they did in the spring, and the cost of a 60 watt bulb for a few hours each evening was negligible in those days. Of course we had to attend to their blackout, and wedge a piece of board over the pop-hole as well as closing the shutters on the window that illuminated the loose box.

We really did everything by the book for our hens, and I must say they repaid us with really tremendous production. One of the little treats we used to give them was a caterpillar-y cabbage or brussels sprout plant, hung up at such a height that they could reach it only by giving a little jump. This was supposed to be good for them because it gave them exercise and prevented them from becoming too fat. It certainly entertained them, and you would see them queueing up to jump at the cabbage, one after the other, until the caterpillars and green leaves were all gone, and all that remained was a white stump and a few picked veins, at which one or two hens would still be hopefully jumping away.

We all had turns at looking after the hens, according to our availability, and, looking back, it is amusing to see how you could deduce who was in charge from the way they tackled the job, and the names the hens got given. Grandma, as I have said, was the first keeper, and her method might be described as super-domestic, with a bit of pet-loving thrown in. She had several favourite hens who got names like 'Lady Jane', who would take corn from her fingers; and she was always trying to think of nice things to put in their mash to make it tasty—but rather the sort of things a human being would like than the foul maggoty specialities that count as *haute cusine* for your average backyard hen.

Thomas and Richard combined forces to look after the second lot of hens (the system being that Rawland removed about half of the old ones each year and provided a compensatory number of pullets), and their management technique might be described as scientific-cum-whimsical. They had an egg production chart stuck up on the kitchen wall which they conscientiously kept filled in, but they knew all the six new pullets as individuals, and gave them all individual names. The names were culled from various military engagements of the American Civil War, on which Thomas was quite an expert; and they did indeed have a decidedly hen-like ring to them. There were Chickamorga, Tala-hatchi, Chattanooga and Chickahominy—and there must have been two others, but I have forgotten them. Those particular pullets were Black Minorcas, and were extremely stylish. They were lightly built, glossy black birds with splashes of white all over them as if they had been thickly spattered by a whitewash brush. But we never had them again because they turned out to be such an unmitigated nuisance. They had Temperament with a capital T, and any unusual noise—a lorry backfiring, a dog barking somewhere near, even a low-flying aircraft—sent them flying in every direction like scraps of burnt paper in a high wind. They were all too capable of surmounting the walls and wire netting that bounded their territory, and then they would hurl themselves, shrieking, into the great outside world. We were always having to go round to Prospect Street to pick up one of our hens, and when we finally cornered it against somebody's dustbin and tucked it under one arm it would yell hysterically all the way home as if it was being stripped of its feathers one by one.

Over the years Rawland provided us with samples of most of the breeds of hen known to man, and, indeed, with many of the crosses. We had white leghorns, black leghorns and brown leghorns; we had Rhode Island reds; we had light Sussex; and, the ones we liked best of all and stuck with whenever he could get them for us, we had Light Sussex crossed with Buff Orping-tons. These were big birds with reasonably neat combs, and their feathers were a pretty warm golden-brown. Their eggs were large and brown, and the generous bowlful we picked up everyday looked particularly sumptuous in that era of stinginess, shortages, and 'doing without'.

Being heavy birds, our hens were a little bit inclined to go broody, and as a broody hen goes out of lay for a considerable time we tried to discourage them from this with every means in our power. We didn't actually call them 'broodies' but used the local term 'clockers' which refers to the sotto voce repetitive clucking noise that a hen makes when her mind is fixed on motherhood. You knew you had a 'clocker' on your hands as soon as you heard this noise coming from a hen that was sitting in one of the nest-boxes when you went to feed the hens in the morning. A hen that was in the box simply to lay its egg might ruffle up its feathers and peck at you if you attempted to slip your hand underneath it, but the steady 'tock! tock! tock!' of the clocker was quite characteristic, and drastic action had to be taken as soon as the condition was diagnosed.

A hen that is intending to hatch out eggs gets a very hot breast, and if you can cool it down you will usually break the spell and abort the broodiness that would otherwise go on for several weeks. And of course a hen that is squatting in a nice straw-lined nest is keeping her breast as hot as possible, as well as hogging a space that other and more active members of society need to lay their eggs in. So our broody hens were removed from the main hen-house and imprisoned instead in an erection called the 'clocking-box' which stood outside the kitchen window, with its back against the projecting wall of the consulting room. There was a rainproof roof on the clocking-box, and it also had solid sides. But the front was slatted, like a coop, and its floor was formed of a large metal grid, of the sort that covers a window area; and as this was propped up on bricks a foot or more off the ground, the accommodation was good and draughty. 'This'll cool her ardour,' we always said conventionally, as we cruelly dragged the burning matron from her warm bed to the airy little-ease of the clocking-box. And it did, usually within two or three days. You were as anxious as the hen to have the whole thing over and done with, for it was a nuisance to have to fill individual food and water pots, and you felt sorry, too, for the poor creature in her uncomfortable exile. So you listened carefully to what she had to say as you attended to her, and the moment that 'tock! tock! tock!' went out of her voice, you let her out and she scampered back to join her sisters, and shortly re-entered the productive life. Sometimes you misjudged it, and found her next morning re-established in a nest-box, clocking, and then the whole thing had to be gone through again; but by and large it worked very well and was well worth the trouble, from our point of view at least.

I had a couple of years as a hen-keeper when I came home from the farm. I had originally intended, on leaving school, to read for a degree in agriculture at Leeds University, and, with this in mind, I did the required year's practical work on a farm in Shropshire. But towards the end of the time I changed my mind and decided instead to try for a place at Oxford, to read English. This took a bit of arranging, because I had to pick up School Certificate Latin, which I hadn't previously taken, as well as having general coaching for the all-important entrance exam. In the event I was lucky because one of my uncles, who was a headmaster in Bradford, very kindly coached me in both Latin and English; but it meant that I had the best part of two years at home, and during that period I looked after the hens.

Having just come back from a large progressive farm I was all hygienic and scientific, and I scrubbed those hens to within an inch of their lives. There was a cold tap with a hose pipe on it in the corner of Elspeth's garage, and every day I scrubbed down the troughs and droppings boards with gallons of cold water and left them outside to 'sweeten' in the wind. I would have liked to remove the litter from the loose box floor and sluice that down too, but I was firmly restrained—the hens needed something to scratch their evening feed of corn around in, I was told, and besides, the dry peat absorbed and de-odorised any droppings that were not caught on the droppings boards.

The real cream of the hen muck that was scraped directly off the droppings boards was put into tea chests in Thomas's garage where it was layered every two or three inches with dried peat and left for a year or so. At the end of that time it had amalgamated with the peat to produce a fine, dry, black powder which made a wonderful top dressing in the garden and had lost all trace of smell and nastiness—indeed, you could never have guessed its origin.

I suppose Papa looked after the hens more than anyone else, and Thomas when Papa was away. Papa, of course, was used to hens and didn't need to look things up in the 'hen book'; we were all pretty used to them before the end and it seemed strange when at last, at the end of food rationing, they were allowed to lapse, and the loose box reverted slowly to garden tools and spiders once again.

EIGHT

PAPA

Though I never met my paternal grandfather, who was sixty-five when Thomas was born, I was lucky enough to know the other one really well, for he came to live with us, and as he was nearly ninety-five when he died, I had the pleasure of his acquaintance well into my adult life.

It was Hitler, in a way, who precipitated the intimacy by arranging for a bomb to destroy Papa's vicarage, for although he remained in the area for a year or two more in a rented house and went on being the vicar of the parish, he was not tempted to stay on in it alone after Dan-dan's death, as I am sure he would have been in his old home.

It was the autumn of 1940 when the vicarage caught its packet and there were seven people in it at the time. Papa, of course, and Dan-dan, already in the early stages of her last illness, Nora, their youngest daughter, Auntie Mary with her children Bruce and Judith, and their father, Uncle Jim, who had come up from London to see his family and ironically enough, to get a rest from the Blitz . . .

It was a long, straggling sort of air raid and at first seemed so uneventful that they didn't even bother to get out of bed in its honour. Dan-dan was ill, Bruce and Judith were sleeping—it seemed a shame to rout them all out and bundle them down to a cold dreary cellar. But the noise of a plane or two droning overhead, the bump! of a bomb in the distance and the flat clatter of the ack-ack guns seemed to indicate that there was a bit of action after all, so they did all go down there and shelter which turned out to have been all for the best.

There were mattresses on the floor for the children and an armchair for Dan-dan; Bruce and Judith promptly fell asleep again. The adults sat and waited. Time ticked by. Mary stood up. 'What we could all do with is a cup of tea,' she said. 'I'll just nip upstairs and make one. Surely they must all have gone by now.' 'Wait, I think I can hear one now,' said Nora. 'Better not go till its passed over.' So they listened in silence as the heavy throb of its engine grew louder and louder and then WOOF the bomb fell, everything went black and their ears clicked with pressure while a fine shower of plaster rained down on their heads and the house shook to its very foundations. Judith woke with a little cry of fear and Mary grabbed her reassuringly. Jim struck a match and lit a candle. Bruce slumbered on. Papa cleared his throat; 'That must have been quite close, choild,' he observed with admirable sang-froid.

It was a long wait till morning. As they sat in the shadowy cellar with the flickering candle, they kept hearing rumbles and thumps from above as the weakened structure collapsed here and there and the masonry showered down. But they were all safe. That was the main thing, though they were all white with shock as well as plaster dust. All except Bruce anyway—his rosy cheek keeping its natural hue beneath a fine powdering of gypsum as he slept undisturbed. Towards morning he awoke, and, immediately, groping in his dressing-gown pocket, dragged out a small aeroplane with which he proceeded to bomb his bed in the most realistic way 'Eeeeow . . . bang! Pow! Crump!' he shouted. 'Look, Daddy, look Papa, I'm a bomber pilot. Eeeeow! Uh-uh-uh-uh-uh—that's the machine guns . . .' He was most surprised and hurt when everybody, nerves jangling, turned on him with one voice and angrily bade him put the beastly thing away.

In the morning the wardens came to dig them out, led by Papa's verger, who almost wept with relief when the whole party stumbled, alive and well, out of their entombment. 'Ee!' he said, over and over again, 'Ee! Thank the Lord! I made sure you could never be alive under all that lot, Vicar! Just look at it!'

And in the lowering light of a grey morning they looked, and a sad sight met their eyes. Bowland vicarage had suffered a death-blow. They could see the vast crater where the bomb had dropped, on the lawn, just five yards beyond the house. The main stonework had held, a fine tribute to the craftsmanship of the Victorian masons who constructed it, but the roof was blown off, the windows were gone, every door was off its hinges, and lumps of plaster lay everywhere, mingled with brick rubble from the internal walls that had collapsed in the blast.

Another house was soon found for Papa and his family and there he lived for a year or two and continued his ministry, but there was no doubt that for him, the word 'home' always meant Boland vicarage. It was a house of so many memories, of course, the house where his children had grown up. Where, for instance, one evening, when he and Dan-dan had been entertaining some friends to dinner, Mary and Elsie had been sent to bed out of the grown-ups' way. Elsie had been tired and had wanted to go to sleep, but Mary had wanted to talk about religion. 'Elsie,' she kept saying 'do you think the Holy Ghost can hear every word we're saying? Do you think the Holy Ghost is in the room now? Elsie! Elsie! Do you think the Holy Ghost . . . ' and so on until eventually Elsie, goaded beyond endurance, snapped out 'Oh, *bother* the Holy Ghost!', put the pillow over her ears and went to sleep. Not so Mary, though; she lay wakeful, scandalised by what she had heard and increasingly fearful of the consequences. Eventually it all got too much for her and she climbed out of bed and pattered downstairs to burst into the dinner-party, a little white-nightgowned, tear-bedabbled figure who sobbed dramatically 'Papa! Elsie's blasphemed the Holy Ghost!'—a crime which, as a good vicar's daughter, specifically, she knew would not be forgiven you!

It was during their time at Boland that Archey, in a family argument, coined his famous proverb: 'Don't judge everybody by the light under your own bushel!' and there, too, where he invented his patent fly-trap. You just took a one pound tin of Tate & Lyle's golden syrup and emptied it on the kitchen table, and soon every fly in the room was struggling in the sticky mess, instead of buzzing about bothering you . . .

As the children grew up they went out into the world, but Nora still lived at home for a while after she started work. She bought a little car and learned to drive it, and it all looked very easy to Papa. So one day, thinking to be helpful, he went, without saying anything, to get the car out of the garage for her, to save her the trouble, and found it wasn't quite as easy as he had expected. He came into the house where Nora was putting on her hat ready to go out, and cleared his throat rather nervously.

'Ha . . . Hm. Nora . . .' he said. 'I'm afraid I've turned your car upside down.' It was true. The car lay neatly outside the garage on its roof, with its wheels in the air looking like a dead dog in a canal. How he did it nobody could ever make out and he himself never saw fit to enlighten us, but it cured him of any wish to drive and he spent the rest of his long life as a passenger.

Dan-dan was already ill when the vicarage was bombed and after her death a year or so later, Papa retired and came to East Gate to live. It was at this stage that he became a canon. But as well as the black rosette to which his new rank entitled him he brought a certain amount of livestock to East Gate with him, to wit, two hives of bees and Prince, his little black mongrel dog.

Prince was a character. In appearance he was not unlike Duchess, the Pomeranian in Beatrix Potter's book *The Pie and the Patty Pan*, except that he was bigger, and his ears turned over at the tips. He was rather a pretty creature, and amiable as well. But he had two faults. For one thing he was musical, and could not resist joining in with excruciating wails if any music reached his ear. And he was pretty catholic, too, in his assessment of what constituted music; it was not just our kind of music, on the gramophone or the wireless, or live, when Richard played the piano. The door bell constituted music, or the telephone; and a passing muffin-man would throw him into uncontrollable ecstasies of improvisation. But—perhaps because of his ecclesiastical background—the thing that always stimulated him to his most strenuous feats of vocal exertion was the sound of the church bells. Now the church in Knearsley, an otherwise unremarkable Victorian building, was endowed with a device called a panotrope, which was a gramophone connected to enormously powerful loudspeakers fixed up in the belfry louvres; and consequently, instead of the three- or four-bell peals that might have been appropriate to such a modest structure, there crashed forth every Sunday records of the greatest peals in the country, amplified to a level that would have put the devil himself to flight. I will at least admit that there was no monotony. Donating a new bell-record became a popular form of memorial in our parish and you never knew from week to week where you were going to find yourself. Westminster Abbey was a popular favourite, with St Paul's a good second; but sometimes we tended southeast for a quick burst of Ely, or introduced our own academic festival with the bells of King's College, Cambridge. I must say *we* all disliked the panotrope, at point blank range as we received it, and it was the one time when we fully sympathised with Prince as he sat on the top lawn, nose pointing skyward, howling in heartbreaking harmony as long as the din lasted.

His best effort was during the war when the liberation of Paris was announced, and the vicar decided that it would be appropriate to relay a record of the Marseillaise. Having failed, however, to track down a recording of this stirring anthem, he was forced to compromise with 'I know that my Redeemer liveth', and Prince sat on a rug in the sunlight and contested it, bar by bar, with a Homerically amplified Isobel Baillie, whose brazen soprano dominated our rejoicings like the very queen of the Valkyries.

Prince's other bad habit was rolling, and although Papa often chastised him for this he never succeeded in breaking him of the weakness. Prince was addicted. He was well aware that his perfume made him unpopular, and he always wore it with the most skulking air and hangdog attitude; but he could not pass up an opportunity of acquiring it, and returned, time and time again plastered with ordure, to meet the cuffs, the reprimands, and the final humiliation of a summary bath, well laced with Dettol. 'Violet', Papa often called him, sarcastically, when he was in a jocular mood or, softening, 'poor old man'. 'The Dear help him, the poor little man,' he would say, in a special bantering voice, rolling him over and rubbing the black furry belly with the toe of his slipper. 'Oh, the Dear help him! He has a terrible, terrible time! The poor little fellow!' Prince loved this and squirmed in ecstasy, his black adoring eyes rolling in his head as he attempted to keep his master's face in focus. But very different was his reception after a good roll. 'Pooh! You've been rolling! Ugh! Ugh! Dirty creature! Disgusting animal!' et cetera et cetera. Unfortunately for Prince the sounds of 'Pooh, rolling!' bore a certain resemblance to the 'Poor old man' of happier confrontations, and you could sometimes see a shade of anxiety cross his face even when he was innocent, if Papa didn't get his intonation just right.

Papa was a Sligo man, and kept his gentle brogue to the end

of his life although far more than half of it was spent in England. His parents were farmers in a fair way of business and had also to begin with a certain interest in a flourishing country mill, but a classic sequence of bad management abetted by drink gradually whittled the property away and Papa's education was striven for, attained, and paid for entirely by his own unaided efforts. He worked as a village schoolmaster for some years and made extra money by correcting exam papers in the evenings. Although he was a young man when he married, and although his children began to arrive when he was still in his early twenties, he managed somehow to support his family and to put himself through Trinity College, Dublin and theological college after that; and the right to put the letters M.A. after his name, being so hard-earned, was always very precious to him.

In one way, despite his long years in industrial Bradford, Papa remained every inch a countryman. Whenever he saw any beautiful or unusual bird, of the sort that makes most of us gasp and reach for the binoculars and the bird book, he had only one reaction. 'Oh!' he would say. 'Would ye look at that! I wish I had me gun!

Papa was a dear man and we were all very fond of him. In his youth he had sovereign-gold hair, but it went white in his twenties so of course he was always white-haired in my recollection. He was of middle height with a clear, rosy skin, blue eyes, and neat features, and his children all inherited from him a particular face-shape with broad, well-modelled cheeks and a short pointed chin redolent of determination. It was not belied by the facts either, I may say, for a more vigorous and determined bunch than the MacNeices I have never met. They got a lot done in whatever walk of life they betook themselves to and to people like me who have missed all those getting-on genes they are a constant source of guilty wonder. How *can* mere mortals be so energetic?

What with his brogue and his strong personality, Papa was splendidly imitable. And imitated he was—by all of us. We felt no pang of conscience about this, for the imitation was done with affection, and never, never in his presence—that would have been unpardonable. As a general rule we felt that the only really important commandment in this whole business of 'doing' people was the eleventh one—'Thou shalt not be found out.' I still believe this really, and I think it adds to our affectionate memory of our grandfather that his rich mellow voice and characteristic gestures are still with us even though he has been dead now for many years.

Papa was a great gesturer and there was a certain ecclesiastical flavour about his hand-waggings, as befitted a churchman. His most characteristic one was a kind of sub-blessing movement, about chest high, executed with the left hand, fingers spread—an attitude that one's hand goes into automatically still whenever one prepares to deliver a remark in his voice.

As he was a Christian and we were all agnostics, there had to be a code of behaviour which, though unwritten, was scrupulously adhered to by both sides while he was living in our house. He did not try to convert us, and we for our part refrained from bending our destructive logic on his sacred cows. As a matter of fact we were glad of his churchgoing because from our point of view it had a useful spin-off. One of his fellow-worshippers had something to do with the Yorkshire C.C.C., and he would often divulge the most fascinating tit-bits of inside information about the players in cosy little post-service chats outside the vestry. We quite looked forward to Papa's return from matins, when he would fill us in on all the latest gossip.

He was a popular man throughout his life and conducted an enormous correspondence. Having lived in the same area for forty years or so he had lots of friends, and one of the advantages of living with us in his retirement was that he was able to see them almost as easily as when he was living in his vicarage at Boland. He had only to walk about five hundred yards up the road to catch the bus or the 'tracklass' down to Bradford, and in the first ten years or so of his retirement he would go down to meet his friends there two or three times a week.

The venue for these meetings was his Masonic Lodge, and the bulk of his friends were other Mason-parsons, collectively known as 'the fellohs'. They played golf together when the weather was fine and snooker when it was wet, and although we rarely met them, we got to know 'the fellohs' quite well by their quoted remarks which were often retailed to us after a good chat session down at the Lodge. 'I was talking to E. this morning,' Papa might say. 'He was telling me he has a recreation ground right by his garden, just like we have here. I was telling him about the trouble we have with the boys. "Boys!" he said, "Mac, don't speak to me about boys! I assure you we're *polluted* with boys at our place!"'

As most of Papa's friends were clergymen, they all shared a particular sense of humour redolent of parish rooms and un-curranty buns, and decorous religious merrymaking which, while going to quite daring and naughty lengths sometimes, still kept within certain bounds which were never, never over-stepped. There were certain subjects that were absolutely sacro-sanct. The clergy was one. 'It's the meanest thing you can do' Papa used to intone sonorously, 'to make jokes about the clergy. They're in the same position as the Royal Family, you see, choild —they can't answer back.' I must say this line never cut very much ice with me—I always thought they were in a better position for answering back than most of us with a captive audience (albeit a small one) for at least ten minutes twice every Sunday. But mine not to reason why, and I was young and fond of Papa anyway so I never really argued the issue. The only people who were permitted to make jokes about the clergy were the clergy themselves, but their efforts in this direction were so laborious that it was hardly worth it in the long run. 'There was a Bishop, and he had a son,' Papa would begin, bobbing up and down on the balls of his feet while the rest of 'the fellohs' clustered around him in attitudes of reverent attention. 'And one winter morning the son came into the room and said "I had a nightmare last night. I dreamt I went to hell." "Oh, and what was it like?" asked the Bishop's chaplain. "Oh, it was just the same as here", replied the young man. "You couldn't see the fire for bloody parsons!"'

I suppose it says something for that story that it has stayed in my mind for thirty years. But of course all Papa's utterances were given a certain extra quality by his delightful brogue and by the resonant timbre of his pulpit voice which pointed up even the most banal observations as a mount does a picture. In the home he was effective, but on his own territory, in church, robed and vested and assisted by a fine Victorian ecclesiastical echo he could be absolutely devastating. 'Marriage was ordained to prevent *forrrnication!*' he thundered at my wedding, while I stood before him with hanging head and shuffling feet and wondered how much he knew and how much he was just imagining.

It was this same trick of delivery that made Papa's non-professional or domestic utterances memorable, although they were often ordinary enough. He was rather given to repeating himself (as we all are, I freely admit) and he often introduced an observation with a trope. 'Nature is woonderful!' he would begin, stretching out his left hand in the classic manner, and would go on to recount some information culled from *John Bull* about the nest-smell of ants or the problems of migrant birds when the sun is overcast. Or he would re-tell a story in exactly the same words as he had often told it in before, a boon to the imitator. 'I had a dog when we were living at Bluestones. You won't remember Bluestones, Elsie.' (A remark always indignantly repudiated, for my mother had been nine, when they left Blue-stones, and remembered it perfectly well.) He bit me. After that I wouldn't hev him in the house.' He was a comfortable person to have about the place because he was so eminently predictable.

But it would be wrong to leave my account of Papa on a note that suggests that he was some kind of buffoon, for he was not. He was most widely loved, and had a most kindly and generous heart. Even after we were grown up and had left home, he would come up to us at the close of every visit when we were getting ready to catch our trains and secretly press into our hands a pound note folded up into a tiny square. 'Get yourself something hot on the journey, choild!' he would murmur, and shuffle conspiratorially away . . .

There was a cloudburst while Papa was playing snooker in the Lodge one day, and when he came out he found that the whole bottom of Bradford was covered by a foot and a half of dirty water, in the middle of which his bus home stood forlornly by its stop like a lodge in a garden of cucumbers.

'What did you do?' we asked him, for he was over eighty at the time. 'Did you get someone to give you a piggy-back?'

'No, I joost rolled up me trouser-legs and hung me boots round me neck and paddled. Then when I got onto the bus I dried me feet wid me pocket handkerchief and put me boots back on,' he replied calmly, and we all had a mental picture of him stalking barefooted through the waste of waters with his boots round his neck and his black canon's hat on his head.

Papa always wore this hat. It was a black homburg with a little black ribbon rosette on the front of it to denote his ecclesiastical rank. He would put it on to feed the hens, or to walk round the garden—even to pay a visit to the outside lavatory, as one of my aunts discovered when she accidentally barged in on him there. 'It's a sight I shall never forget,' she told me afterwards. 'Papa sitting there, so dignified, reading the *Church Times*, with his Canon's hat on his head and his trousers round his ankles.'

Doctors, dealing with bodies, are naturally freer in their speech and broader in their humour than clergymen, who are preoccupied with souls. (Psychiatrists presumably come somewhere in the middle.) Our house was littered with reminders of mortality, from the skull on the top of the cupboard by the stairs, to the foetus in a bottle of spirit that stood on one end of the Welsh dresser in the hall. One might have expected that Papa would object to the fact that these relics were kept rather as curiosities than anything else and were certainly treated with levity rather than reverence if the occasion arose. Hats might be dumped on the skull's pate out of the way or a rose thrust facetiously between its teeth; there was certainly no anxiety about the fact that it had once belonged to a human being who had had a soul, nor worry about the fact that it was not buried in consecrated ground. It was a woman's skull, and eventually Thomas covered it with plasticine and made it into a head which bore a surprising and entirely fortuitous resemblance to one of my aunts.

The feotus was perhaps an even more unexpected ornament and had an even dimmer personality. Indeed it even occurred to us one dinner time that we had no idea whether it was a male or a female, in spite of the fact that it had sojourned with us for many years. Richard got up from his place and went out into the hall to investigate but returned almost at once, looking dissatisfied. 'The wretched little beggar's got its hands over it,' he said.

In the matter of humour as well as of religion there had to be a certain amount of restraint when Papa was present. We enjoyed a touch of Rabelais in our jokes but he toed a much stricter line. 'Unsavoury' was his all-embracing term of derogation for anything he considered a bit too near the knuckle—or rather, 'oonsavoury', because of his Irish accent. The nearest he ever got to telling a dirty joke was at Christmas dinner one year, when he told us that archaeologists had been puzzling over the function of a recently excavated ceramic vessel which even the best informed experts had failed to identify until they noticed an incised inscription round its neck. He wrote out the inscription on the back of his place card and passed it round the table. It read 'ITI SAPIS POTAN DA BIGO NE'. Not bad for a C. of E. parson of over eighty. I wonder where he got it from? It may have come from one of 'the fellohs' or he might even have read it in *John Bull*, a publication which he endowed with an almost Biblical authority.

Papa's ideas about what was 'oonsavoury' did not always coincide with those of his grand-children, and on one occasion he gave Bruce, my cousin, one of the most embarrassing ten minutes of his life. Bruce, who was thirteen or so, was studying *Macbeth* at school and had been unlucky enough to be chosen for the part of Lady Macbeth in the classroom read-through that was part of the study. He was complaining at home of the dreadful nature of some of the words that were thus put into his mouth, but he would have done better to keep it shut. Papa was staying with them at the time and he rode roughshod over all Bruce's talk of self-consciousness. 'Pooh! Pooh! choild, you don't know what you're talking about, great nonsense, give me the book here . . .' and there and then in the kitchen he insisted on declaiming all the worst passages in his most sonorous pulpit voice with a wealth of pantomimic gesture while Bruce averted his eyes and tried to think of other things yet still look politely attentive.

> I have given sook, and *know* what 'tis
> To loove the babe that milks me . . .
> I would while it was smiling in me face
> Have plooked me nipple from its bawnless gooms
> and *dashed* its *brains* out . . .

and so on and so forth. Poor Bruce.

Not but what Bruce was rather easily embarrassed at this period of his life. I remember him once absolutely refusing to go up to the grocer's shop with a list that had the word 'Sanilav' on it. 'I couldn't possibly say that *aloud*', he protested. 'Well, you could just pass the list over the counter and let the girl read it,' suggested Auntie Mary. 'No, no,' moaned Bruce, 'she might read it out loud and that would be just as bad. Everybody would look at me and laugh.'

Papa was quite a reader. As well as devouring *John Bull* from cover to cover every week he would read anything else that came his way—like the rest of us in that, for we were a great family for reading. The house was full of books and there wasn't a single room without a bookcase in which the books were piled with a total absence of system. Papa had a four-sided revolving bookcase in his bedroom with the usual arbitrary selection of reading matter in it. *Bright Day* by J. B. Priestley separated Baxter's Bible from *I was Hitler's Maid*, while a medical text book, Hermann's *Difficult Labour*, leaned confidingly against a nineteenth-century book of sermons. You could have said that Papa's reading tastes were catholic.

Not that Papa himself would ever have used that word in its dictionary sense of 'universal'. For him 'Catholic' had only one meaning and it was one that brought the light of battle to his eye. But he would not say 'Catholic', *tout court*, even so. 'Call them *Roman* Catholics!' he would insist, chuckling with Protestant glee. 'They *hate* it!'

In spite of the vast numbers of books in the house we were all always chronically short of reading matter. For our literary life was conducted rather on the same principle as the sea anenome's, which sits on a rock with spread tentacles and makes do with whatever the sea wafts into its reach. It was thus with our books. Birthdays or Christmas would see a vast influx of book-presents from everyone to everyone else, and between whiles we depended on odd purchases made for journeys, or borrowed from other branches of the family living in the area.

Sometimes a book would appear that everyone wanted to read at the same time, and then a covert and undeclared warfare would break out, with everyone trying to acquire the coveted volume and abstract it for a quiet half-hour's read and everyone else trying to thwart them. One such book which captivated everybody's fancy was Boswell's *London Journal*, which went from hand to hand like the baton in a relay race, and which Papa was as keen as any of us to get hold of. His cloth, however, was somewhat of an inhibition to him in the open pursuit of his ends; for he obviously felt a touch of self-consciousness, as a clergyman, in being seen to be looking for a work which had a somewhat spicy reputation. But he did want to get his hands on it all the same, and he finally compromised by refusing to name it and referring to it always, in his search, as 'That Book'. 'Have you seen That Book, choild?' he would enquire anxiously as he saw Thomas's back disappearing into his morning surgery, and I would take pity on him and fetch it for him from the settle in the hall where Thomas had been reading it for a quarter of an hour while he was supposed to be doing up his shoes.

An even more awkward problem arose for Papa with the publication of a book called *The Trials of Karl Fuchs* which was another one that we all wanted to read. It was not so much the matter in this case as the name, for he could never frame his soft palate to the guttural German sound, and an unsuccessful attempt could sound so unfortunate coming out of a mouth above a dog-collar. But after a few boss shots he bethought himself of the formula that had stood him in good stead on the previous occasion, and when he began referring to the unhappy traitor as 'That Man', we didn't pretend that we didn't know who he meant.

A few years later the problem cropped up again when Sir Vivian Fuchs spent a whole winter in the news as he struggled bravely across Antarctica, but by now Papa had had enough of circumlocution. Feeling perhaps too tired by now to invent a new formula, he settled for calling him 'Foosh', and 'Foosh' he remained for all of us to the end of the chapter.

NINE

THOMAS

Thomas, my father, was a doctor and a very good one, but those who know him best have always felt that by going in for medicine he missed his true vocation. He should really have been a don.

He would have been, too, had it not been for the Great War. He was already embarked on the way. He had gone up to Pembroke College, Cambridge, to read Ancient History, and I am sure that one thing would have led to another. No doubt he would have taken a first, and an academic career would have followed by a natural progression—which would have been very nice for him. But since he would not have met my mother, we children would never have been born, so for us there would have been disadvantages.

In any case, it was not to be. At the end of his first year he was called up, and when he returned from the army he had changed his mind. So instead of going back to Cambridge and Ancient History, he went to Leeds and read Medicine, and, being an exceptionally able man, he sailed through that without any trouble at all. And we were born.

He began to show that he was going to be clever when he was quite young. He and his sister, Phyllis, who is three years his junior, have exactly the same kind of mind, and together they created a world of fantasy not unlike that made by the Brontë children, but satirical rather than heroic in genre, and populated by real people, developed and expanded as the game demanded.

They were both good with words, with prehensile memories for the felicitous phrase or the tit-bit of chance-heard conversation. One example came from Thomas's school when he was about eight, when the master rebuked a boy for taking a swipe at another during the Latin lesson. 'What on earth do you think you're playing at, Binks?' he demanded angrily. Binks turned round. He was an angelic-looking child like a choirboy, and his round blue eyes brimmed with outrage as he raised them to the master's, and explained his sudden burst of aggression. 'Oh, sir!' he replied. 'He scandalised me! He said my face was like a cat's bottom—turned inside out and *whitewashed*!'

Nor were they alone in having a good ear for a quotation. Uncle James, one of Grandma's high-spirited brothers, was a man who remembered sayings, and one that he collected is still often quoted in the family. It was a rainy evening, and he was driving home from work. As he bowled along he passed a workman trudging along the road carrying a bag of tools, and, being a kindly man, he pulled up and offered him a lift. The man climbed into the dog-cart and lit his clay pipe; Uncle James whipped up the mare and away they went towards Leeds. After a few exchanges about the rain and the mare's paces, conversation languished, and more for the sake of saying something than for any other reason, Uncle James pointed with his whip at a building they were passing, and observed 'That's the chapel I go to.' The man removed his pipe from his mouth. 'Oh, aye?' he said politely. 'Well, of coorse, Ah'm not a chapel booger meself. But Ah've nowt against them as is!'

If people obliged with good sayings it was helpful; but in the vast mythology that Tom and Phyllis created it didn't much matter, the sayings were provided if necessary. Characters originating in real people—relations or acquaintances—were developed in poems, songs, and plays to a pitch where their very mothers would have failed to recognise them and the resultant pool of personalities acted out dramas rather like the sketches we see now on television, but often a good deal more scurrilous. Clergy formed a particularly rich seam. Their parents both being religious, Tom and Phyllis attended a lot of services and had plenty of opportunity to observe both vicars and curates performing their professional parts. So a range of local clergy got absorbed into the folklore and emerged into the fantasy world fearfully and wonderfully changed. Each had his own accent and his own mannerisms, and behaved in accordance with his own personality in the endless proliferation of stories that made up the Horner myth.

There was Mr M., for instance, a vicar. He had a way of

97

breaking up his words as if they were hyphenated, and he also pronounced the letter 's' as 'f', 'becaufe,' he explained, 'I learnt to read from a ve-ry old book.' In real life as vicar of a large parish he had several curates under him, and in the myth they emerged as a terrible gang. They were depicted as a set of would-be rakes who were always out on the town except when they were actually under the immediate eye of their master, who did not hesitate to chastise them whenever he found them at fault. One little poem from Mr M. to Mr H. demonstrates this facet of their relationship:

> Now, Mr H., where 'ave you been?
> Thif eve-ning you were not in chu'ch.
> A little dinner at the Queen'f?
> I thought af much! I thought af much!

> You've 'ad fome whifky with your Schweppef;
> You look a fpectacle of woe!
> You've been thrown down the Empire ftepf?
> I told you fo! I told you fo!

> I know your 'ead if feeling bad—
> You know that I've a large, flat 'and;
> Come to my ftudy, Mr H.—
> You underftand, you underftand!

Mr M. was supposed to acquire his curates at a curate fair and, being an experienced vicar, he sometimes came home with some very good bargains. As in horse-coping, there were certain rules that you were wise to observe if you were looking for a useful curate at the cheap end of the market, and Mr M. was dead set against a curate with bad feet. 'No fallen archef and no varicofe veinf,' he would insist, 'but a flight fpavin doefn't matter, af long af it'f not in an important plafe.' A high-class curate slightly touched in the wind was the best thing to look for if you were really after a bargain, but here again you were taking a risk, and you need real expertise to keep out of trouble. A 'whistler' was one thing, and not very bad in a provincial parish, though he might not have been acceptable to a London congregation, but a roarer would not do anywhere, and you were well advised to give your prospective purchase a good trot out before getting him into the pulpit and listening to a sample of his delivery.

98

For there were sharks in the curate-dealing world, and all manner of faults might be smoothed over. A good piece of butter slipped down his throat would conceal broken wind in a curate; and likewise there were powders that could be administered to make a dozy curate seem lively or a savage one quiet. And there were other tricks too, as old as the hills, that the unscrupulous could have recourse to which would leave you right out of pocket if you did not know how to look out for yourself.

Mr M. was caught once like this. In a moment of weakness he allowed a dealer to buy him a drink in a pub and, as one thing led to another, he ended up very drunk indeed and got home disgracefully late and with no memory at all of the latter part of the day. He found out in the morning just what he'd been up to, and the knowledge filled him with dismay. For when he came down to the kitchen he discovered that he had accidentally purchased an enormous coal-black curate who didn't speak a word of English, or, indeed, of French or German, or any language of which Mr M. had even a smattering. It was all very awkward.

The awkwardness was compounded by the fact that the congregation was expecting, the next Sunday, to hear the new curate preach, and there was no way in which Mr M. could explain the dilemma without admitting his own fault, which he was unwilling to do. So he stooped to a subterfuge. By a lucky chance the pulpit in his church was a large one and there was quite a lot of room underneath it in which a man could sit concealed—or several men, for that matter. So, making use of this feature, Mr M. laid his plans. The black curate was instructed to get up into the pulpit and open and close his mouth as if preaching, at the appropriate time. And Mr H. was to be secreted with a torch in the space under the pulpit, and was to read aloud one of Mr M.'s old sermons which, it was hoped, the congregation would not recognise, thus getting over the difficulty and leaving the way open for the unwanted bargain to be exchanged for something more useful at the next curate fair.

But he had reckoned without Mr H. He, still smarting from a recent chastisement over some trifling crime, like consecrating two whole bottles of communion wine, saw an opportunity of revenge, and laid his plans too, to confound his poor master.

When he went to his place under the pulpit before the service he did not go alone. He took two other curates, Mr D. and Mr G., in with him, and a whole volume of sermons. And instead of just one sermon lasting, say, twenty minutes, those naughty curates preached in relays and went on for four hours, while the congregation fidgeted, the vicar sweated in his stall, and the poor black curate stood there opening and shutting his mouth obediently until he was nearly dropping with fatigue.

It compounded the pleasure of these fantastic inventions that the real live Mr M. often came to tea with one of his curates— Mr H., Mr D. or Mr G. as chance might have it—and Phyllis and Tom, passing tea-cakes as if butter wouldn't melt in their mouths, could exchange bland knowing glances and hug themselves at the thought of the reverend gentlemen cavorting so splendidly in that other life that they led, knowing absolutely nothing about it.

There was a certain element of danger in the game because there was always the chance that one of the victims might somehow get hold of a work of art in which he was featured, an eventuality which would have put the cat squarely in the middle of the pigeon flock. But it only happened once. An uncle-by-marriage picked up a poem about himself by Phyllis in the Hiawatha metre, which described his behaviour at some feast where at first he pretended to have no appetite and only picked at the food.

> Only trifled with his victuals
> Making out he was not hungry
> Till the savoury steam assailed him
> And his greed at last oe'rcame him,
> And his arms moved like steam-engines
> And he feasted in good earnest.

'Rather cheeky, don't you think?' he enquired, in his own much-imitated voice and accent, waving the incriminating document, and Phyllis, red with mortification, snatched it out of his hand and rushed away and burned it. The fragment quoted above, which happened to be lodged in her mind, is all that remains of that unfortunate poem.

As a family we have always had a frivolous streak, looking for something to laugh at and noticing incongruities. If funny things don't happen to us on our way to the theatre it does not make very much difference. We have ways of making ourselves laugh, and several games that we still play have come down from Tom and Phyllis's childhood. They depend almost always on chance word-associations and in that, bear some slight relationship to 'Consequences', but they are quicker and easier to play, and do not require the presence of so many players to make them work.

The first game of this kind that they developed was from a book they had which was a biography of some famous boxer. It must have been dull indeed as it was published, for it gave blow-by-blow accounts of all his fights and omitted no detail, unto the least jot and tittle. But it was splendid basic material. One of them would read it aloud, substituting two of their characters for the boxers, and stopping whenever they reached a word which denoted any part of the body. The other had a copy of Gray's *Anatomy*, which they opened at random, and supplied the missing word with the first part of the body they came across in that classic work. And the contests thus described were not dull at all. One might read:

There was a deathlike hush in the vast auditorium as Uncle X danced out of his corner. His massive opponent, Mr M. (the vicar) seemed twice his height and bulk, and the crowd gasped as the first punches were thrown. Mr M. struck first with a straight right aimed at Uncle X's uvula, but the coccyx of the smaller man swayed out of the way and the glove only brushed his navel. He was quick to retaliate. Feinting with his right he lured his big opponent within his reach and then struck hard, two left jabs to the Achilles tendon. Maddened, the larger man lowered his armpit and charged in like a maddened bull throwing punches in all directions. A flurry of blows caught Uncle X on the buttock and he was driven back on the ropes. But with a quick twisting movement, like an eel, he ducked under the other's tongue and connected with an uppercut right on the point of the large bowel.

And so on and so forth.

There was another game in which words were written on scraps of paper and jumbled up, according to their kinds, in a series of containers and then drawn forth into a formula. One lot was names, one actions, and one places; then there were three sections for clothes and another for accessories. Then you fitted it all together in a framework and came up with something that could be very silly indeed. 'I saw Hitler, paddling at Potsdam', averred one of them I happen to remember, 'wearing an enormous tweed robe, and carrying a cracked duck.'

We would sometimes vary this by snipping words and phrases from newspapers and trying to make headlines and you did get some that made you wish you could read the article they referred to. 'Sterilized vagrant scared to marry' was one which suggested a splendid range of possibilities.

But although we could all play these simple games there were heights where we late-comers never aspired to tread, and the ultimate difficult art form, invented by Thomas and successfully practised only by him, was the Square Tale. This, as its name implies, was a short story in two dimensions, that could be read either straight across, like ordinary prose, or in columns, vertically. It is easy to start a square tale and not too hard to do the first few lines. But to finish it so that it makes something approaching sense in both directions is most damnably difficult even with the latitude of puns, slang, and occasional uncolloquial usages. Indeed as far as I know (and there may be other Square writers that have pulled it off without my knowledge), it has only been achieved twice, which is a pity, for a good square tale is a wonderful breeding ground for a whole range of quotable phrases.

My favourite square tale is about Pa. Pa was a late addition to the family, being Grandma's second husband, and although I can form no opinion of him from personal experience, as he died in the year I was born, I must say that his step-children received him with mixed feelings and responded to his superficial bonhomie with a good many reservations. So we can infer that he was not a heart of oak, though he did make good character-fodder being a great individual in both voice and delivery. He had a high, weary, complaining tone of voice, with a marked Yorkshire accent, and his phraseology abounded with quirks of the sort that make imitations instantly recognisable. He said 'P'raps' and 'of coorse' very often, usually transposing their meanings, and began most of his sentences with a plaintive 'Why . . .' 'Why, I think of coarse old England's doone,' he would say, or 'I think p'raps we shall all die, and of coarse we shall all be buried.' Or he would tell a little anecdote, as 'Why, Josh 'artley and Jim and me was walking along the street and we passed the 'otel Metropole and they said shall we go in and I said nay, so of coorse we did.' I have left out the punctuation on purpose because that was how he spoke—all in a straight line on his one high creaking note.

He was quite a rich man and the source of his wealth was a fortunate accident that he had the good sense and business acumen to take advantage of. In the beginning he was a quarry owner (he pronounced quarry to rhyme with marry, and had an eye always lifting for a nice bit of stone—it was he who pointed out to us the beautiful workmanship in the stonework of our own house), and he did well enough, but was not in the big league, though comfortable. And he blasted away at his quarry and sold the stone till the seam ran out and he thought he was going to be left lamenting. But it was not to be. Behind the workable stone lay a thick band of deposit in two distinct layers, still well inside his land where he owned all the mineral rights, all neatly laid out and nicely exposed by the quarrying just waiting to be worked and made into money. The top layer was finest brick-earth and the bottom layer first quality coal. So he set up a brick-works instead of a stone-works and prospered exceedingly.

He and Grandma liked travelling both in England and abroad, and Pa, in the expansive phase of his prosperity, felt no touch of self-consciousness under the supercilious eyes of the waiters in the big five-star-type hotels he favoured. He had the brass, after all, and it was their job to understand what he wanted, and if he didn't say it right it was their fault, wasn't it, for writing the menu in such a damned silly foreign lingo. So he ploughed on and to this day we all still pronounce petit pois 'peetitt poys' in his memory. On another occasion in Scotland he puzzled the waiter who asked him in a broad Glasgow accent 'What soup, sir?' Pa, thinking he had said 'What to sup?', creaked cheerily 'Why, ginger ale, to be sure!' only realising by the consternation of the man's honest countenance that he had misunderstood the question.

103

Tom and Phyllis were grown up by the time he became their stepfather, so they did not get too oppressive a dose of his company; and he did try to be cordial within the limits of his personality. Thomas was by then a doctor and Phyllis was engaged to George who was a barrister, and so Pa conscientiously worked up a bit of medical conversation for one and a legal story for the other and delivered them straight away, politely, whenever he met them, before going on to talk about subjects nearer his heart, like quarries or peetitt poys or the advantages of total abstention. They were both quite short pieces. In the medical bit he would describe an affliction that had occasioned the death of one of his friends and ask for a snap diagnosis. 'Why Tom, it appears that in the case of poor Mr Craven it was his bowils that were the trouble. It appears they should have been like this' (demonstrating a gnarled hand, the fingers spread out widely) 'and instead they were like this' (the fingers curled slowly and ended up as a tightly clenched fist). 'What would that be, Tom?'

In the legal story for George there was a regular opening formula. 'Why George, it appears that even lawyers can be voolgar. Because when we was 'aving our lawsuit with Ben Gill about the quarry, we 'ad to seek learned counsel's opinion. And we 'ad to take all the evidence to 'im and let 'im sort it out for 'imself. And he looked through it, and what do you think 'e said? 'E said Take it away, Mr A, 'e said, it isn't worth pissing on! Aye, it appears even lawyers can be voolgar!'

Pa's own two sons were another George and Herbert, both of whom are now dead, and the plot of the square tale is an absolutely apocryphal account of the arrangements they made for his funeral. It is actually true that Pa's body did burst before it could be screwed discreetly into a coffin and it may be that his spirit sent messages 'from function on pleasant height of heaven' but all the rest is invention.

Thomas wrote other things besides square tales. He could rhyme with the facility of a W. S. Gilbert and he also composed the music for two or three operettas. He draws and paints like an angel too and his works are often illustrated. He and Phyllis used to make cardboard marionettes of their characters and do scurrilous plays with them in a model theatre they had; the costumes varied according to the exigencies of the action, and were usually grossly inappropriate to the real person. As time went on, people tended to get stuck with one particularly silly kind of gear in which they always depicted thereafter, and the incongruity was thereby increased. Uncle X, for instance, always appeared dressed as a page boy, his skinny chest caving under rows of brass buttons, and his lugubrious face with its drooping moustachios gazing out despairingly from under a jaunty pill-box hat. He, perhaps more than any of the other characters, has remained current and fresh accounts of his misdeeds still trip freely from the ready pen of his chronicler. Or perhaps I should say chroniclers. For Phyllis has written nearly as many Uncle X poems as Thomas has, both alone and in partnership with George, her husband, and George himself was once moved to do a splendid legal poem about him which broke new ground in a perfect spate of Norman French. A cousin in America, Joyce, contributes the occasional short piece; he is very much a family hero.

Being a family doctor worked out very well for a man of Thomas's wide-ranging talents. Inspiration could be jotted down between visits on the back of his list, and he even painted occasionally in the intervals between a measles, a mumps, and an 'ee, it's me leg again, doctor'. I remember one day passing him on my bike as he sat in his car perfectly absorbed, with his watercolour box open on the seat beside him and a sketch-pad on the steering wheel, splashing down a quick impression of a particular light-effect over the valley which he wanted to remember. He did not even see me.

In his reading he is entirely catholic, reading what came his way and adding it to the enormous store of knowledge he carries round in his head. But he has several specialities. He is probably as well-informed as anyone in the country on the American Civil War, and the Peninsular campaigns of Wellington have also been of particular interest to him. There is some doubt as to the actual date of Wellington's birth but the date that used to be allocated to him is also Thomas's birthday, which may have something to do with this particular feeling of fellowship. After all, they are both Taureans.

Cricket is another of Thomas's interests and again he is a perfect walking Wisden with his encyclopaedic memory. As a young man he was good enough to have a trial for Yorkshire, and that was Yorkshire in the height of its glory when you had to be good indeed to get a regular place. He has always been a member of the Y.C.C.C., and when I lived at home in my late teens it was the pleasure of my life to go to county matches with him. I would go by myself quite often too and I can't think of a better cheap day's entertainment. The bus fare to the ground was fourpence (I was glad when it went up; it always seemed something of a risk to say to a big strong conductor 'Will you give me a fourpenny one, please') and entrance to the ground and the pavilion, with the lady's ticket from his membership card, were free. It was twopence for a match card and ninepence for a little hired cushion to keep the pangs of the slatted seats away from your bottom. Food came from home, in the form of sandwiches, and drink was a flask of hot coffee or a bottle of lukewarm orange squash as seemed more appropriate according to the weather. It was all quite idyllic in the great, green-striped grounds, with the stately white-clad figures and the sun filtering bravely through the lowering industrial haze above. Sometimes Thomas would finish his visiting list early enough to come and spend a couple of hours in the afternoon, when we would leave half an hour before the end because he had to be back in time for evening surgery.

I enjoyed cricket in any circumstances, but it was twice as entertaining if I was with Thomas because he could perceive the strategy of the game and tell me what was going on. Bowlers set traps for different batsmen, according to their weaknesses, and you got to know what they would be trying to do as you watched the team with Thomasian commentary regularly through a couple of seasons. Cyril Washbrook of Lancashire and England, for instance, was a great hooker, and the bowlers tried to tempt him with short-pitched balls outside the leg stump. Only one in an over, of course; it didn't do to be too obvious. You had to resign yourself to the fact that he would get a couple of fours or even sixes off your bait balls, but you had your revenge. A fielder who had been placed on the long leg boundary was instructed to 'creep' a little each over, and often enough he would get round without being noticed and dismiss the batsman with a catch at deep square leg.

Thomas started watching cricket at the beginning of the

century and had seen all the old heroes. He had stories about them too—about Mitchell, for instance, the Yorkshire opening bat in the years before the war, who could stonewall so dourly that the game died on its feet and the bowlers raved impotently at his bland and impassive defence. It was the Roses Match at Old Trafford in 1938 and the Lancashire attack was keen. But Mitchell at his sourest was not to be dislodged and he met everything with the deadest of bats and attempted no scoring strokes till the crowd was both bored and disgusted. At last a man stood up on the popular side of the ground, turned his back on the game and addressed his fellow spectators. He was a natural Stentor and he said what they'd all been thinking—and said it loudly. 'Ivry bloody year!' he exclaimed, 'yon chap cooms 'ere and spoils t'Bank 'oliday!' There was a murmur of agreement and, encouraged, he went on. 'Us lads at Wigan 'as gotten us 'olidays, and my Missus says so to me this morning, "Why, Joe, whears ta bahn today?" and I says to 'er "Ah'm bahn t'Owd Trafford to see t'match" ah says "and what shall Ah see? Bloody Mitchell!" ' He turned round and addressed the players and his big voice floated out over the shaven turf to the white-flannelled figures in the middle. 'Eh, Mitchell!' he roared. 'Ah've summat ter tell thee, and tha needn't pretend tha can't 'ear me, 'cas tha can! Ivry bloody year for nigh on ten year tha's coom 'ere and spoilt t'Bank 'oliday. But there's bahn ter be a war, and tha wean't be 'ere t'next year, nor t'year after it, and what I say is Thank God for it! So, Good Afternoon, and booger yer!' with which he made a splendid exit and was clapped all the way to the gate. Even now when somebody says to me 'Good afternoon' with a shortened, North country 'a', I have to fight down an urge to add, usually with no relevance whatsoever, 'and booger yer!'.

People often stood up during cricket matches and shouted remarks; it was all part of the thing. Sometimes they were funny, but usually they were silly and boring and often enough were from drunks. There was one I remember who was a particular pest. He was sitting next to Thomas, and throughout the day he kept up a constant barracking of advice and correction with a throat made of leather which he continually oiled from three quart flagons he had brought in with him in an old paper bag.

107

Various people told him to sit down and shut up but he wouldn't, and as time went on and the level in the flagons dropped lower he got more and more aggressive. Thomas was nearly driven wild. Like a high-mettled horse goaded into a fury he sat there with eyes flashing, nostrils distended and fists clenched, but in spite of his irritation he controlled himself nobly and spoke not a word. You could see the pressure mounting in the boiler though, and at last he began to tremble all over with rage as he did when he was really incensed—a sign that should have been a warning that the needle had soared well past the red mark indicating danger and that all wise men should seek cover and the wicked cease from troubling. But our little friend was too far gone for prudence and turned round to this fearsome sight with the utmost blandness. Sitting there like a moulting sparrow beside an eagle he looked his big neighbour coolly up and down. 'There's no need to sit there beside me tremblin','" he said, and tapped his own chest, a sharp, self-congratulatory blow. 'I aren't tremblin'!'" Whereupon he got up and left leaving us with stretched nerves and another quotation.

Although Thomas has always been able to drive, he is not a natural mechanic and has never felt tempted to do jobs on his own car when it needs its plugs cleaning or its engine tuning or what have you. Before the war he used to change his car once a year, so his lack of sympathy with its internal problems did not matter too much, but from 1939 onwards cars were hard to get and he had to make each one last much longer, and this did lead to some troubles which he coped with in his own most individual way.

There was one car I particularly remember because it was so heavy. It was a bad starter and could only be jerked into life by a bump-start down a hill, particularly first thing in the morning, when its engine was cold. We developed a regular drill. At the first sight of Thomas, list in hand, emerging from the house those of us who were on regular pushing fatigue dropped whatever we were doing, and rushed to our duty. Then we lined ourselves up each in her allotted position and got to work. There were three of us—Ardar our secretary, Mrs W. our daily, and me—and before we could get the car to the start of its downhill run, we had to push it up a little slope just outside the garage.

Thomas was able to help with this bit so it wasn't too bad, but there was another long push of fifty or sixty yards on the level when he had to sit in it ready, and we women were on our own. It was not hard, really, of course, for three strapping women to push along a car on the level, even a big car with quite a big man in it, but I was always nearly rupturing myself with inward giggles at the ridiculousness of the scene. There sat Thomas with his noble head and aquiline countenance, high on the driving-seat steering for dear life—and his little gang of female slaves in their overalls pushed and grunted as the car moved slowly along—till at last the road tilted, gravity started, and we fell, puffing, behind. Once he was over the crest he had plenty of chance to bump-start for the road sloped downhill for four miles, and as a final dispensation of providence there was a garage just at the end of the slope. So, on the few occasions when he absolutely *couldn't* raise a spark out of his engine he used the last fading impulse of his coasting to roll onto their forecourt and they always managed to get him mobile again one way or another.

Thomas's individuality as a driver did not stop with his starting technique. He had other games that he played and if the car didn't like it, that was too bad. Some days he would decide to try to get round the practice without ever changing gear, and by dint of starting always on a downhill slope and ignoring the engine's screams and groans as it laboured, he would sometimes achieve it, and spend a whole day in third or even top—quite an achievement in as hilly an area as ours, albeit terribly hard on the car. He had various amenities too in his cars that were useful if not elegant—like a pipe-rack made from a twisted steel knitting needle sticking out from the dashboard—and his own way of dealing with breakages, which sometimes almost called for a new section to be written into the highway code. If you had been driving behind the red car, which was a heap, for example, you might have been puzzled for a moment as the window opened and a long stick with a big pad of lint and cotton-wool fastened to its end with sticking plaster was slowly extended into your view. You need not have worried. In our district the signal had a meaning which was well understood by all those who were likely to be driving behind Thomas on a wet day. 'I Am Going to Wipe My Windscreen' it implied, and, sure enough, as soon as it was far enough out it bent round to the front and did just that, the windscreen wiper being broken, and Thomas somehow never seeming to have time to take it in to be seen to . . .

But if Thomas was not much of a mechanic he deserves recognition for one thing which I now for the first time disclose with much pride. He won the war. Single-handed he did it, weaving magic in the bathroom, and historians of the future may correct the books if they have a mind to, for after years of modest concealment all will now be revealed.

It was a damp patch that began it. High up on the wall it kept growing and growing, and the glossy cream paint would go brown and discoloured even when it was touched up. It was ugly. So Elspeth said to him one day 'Tommy, why don't you take your oil paints and do a nice mural on the end wall of the bathroom to cover up that nasty brown patch?', and he did.

He was in there all of one Sunday, fed, at intervals through the door, and nobody was allowed to see the picture till it was completed. And we all waited in pleasant anticipation and discussed what it might be, looking forward to the beauty that we were sure would greet our eyes when the artist emerged. What would it be? Elspeth thought perhaps a landscape, with bare trees and fields, and a range of rolling hills marching away into the distance. Gillian said perhaps a sea scape with tossed clouds and wave-crests and perhaps a ship or two. But they were both wrong.

For when at last we were allowed in, there, striding across the wall, was a monster. More than life-size it towered up to the top of the wall where its great eagle's head, beak agape, was surmounted by a crown. Its huge crimson wings were spread wide; dominating the top half of the wall; from the waist down it was a man, and its great legs, the colour of dried blood, strode conqueringly across a fantastic landscape. Green and orange half-circles receded behind it to a curious cubist city in the distance. We all looked in some awe. It was difficult to know what to say. You could hardly remark 'how nice!'. But before long Elspeth found her voice. 'Well!' she said, 'it certainly covers up the damp patch very effectively!'

How the war was affected by the mural may not yet be clear.

But a start had been made. One day a year or two later it occurred to Thomas that the emblem of Germany was an eagle, and that perhaps from a superstitious point of view it was not a good thing to have one strutting in triumph before conquered territories all over your bathroom wall. So he bought himself another tube of dark red paint and set about putting it right. And when we went in for our baths that evening a great change had taken place. Gone were the great striding legs and the attitude of lordly domination; gone was the kingly crown. Instead, the eagle flapped its wings in its death throes, knocked backwards in flight by a fatal blow from an unseen hand. Its legs—ordinary bird's legs this time—were drawn up to its body in a convulsion of agony, and an arrow, deep in its body, sent a scatter of blood down the wall to a realistic pool at the bottom . . .

And it worked. Less than a month later came the battle of El Alamein which has always seemed the hinge or turning-point of the war, and with our eagle bleeding and dying, Germany weakened and faded and the Allies invaded Sicily, Italy, and eventually moved on to the costly triumphs of D-Day.

We congratulated Thomas on his successful sympathetic magic and Elspeth told him he had better take the Japanese war in hand too. So he went in again and a loathsome picture emerged of a Japanese in the very act of committing hara-kiri just where the bird's original legs had been, between the towel rail and the floor. That worked too.

We of course got very used to these pictures. After the first few remarks on their magical quality—always intended to be frivolous—we hardly noticed them, and apart from the fact that they did cover up the damp spots they might as well have not been there. But it was amusing to see the dubious looks on the faces of any strangers who had occasion to go into our bathroom at this curious representation of death and despair, blood, blades and bowels all over the wall. So we used to have to explain the mystical potency of the images to them and we would finish off by saying 'But of course if you have a medicine man in the house, this is the sort of thing you have to put up with.'

THE SQUARE TALE

George	said	Dr Ewe	one	day	your	Pa	is
in	need	of	extreme	unction	undertaker	is	needed
search	not	Rothwell	to	day	but	cast away	all thought
of	worry	for	another	comes	whose	great	power
thrills	us	Mr Bence	the	parson	who	I say	having
crept	upstairs	secretly	holy	rites	will	be	celebrated
into	the bargain	soon	Dr Ewe	Thunders	tell	your	relatives
Pa's	has	departed	keens	Herbert	grave	sorrow	in this
chamber's	been	Dr Ewe	for dear	night	has	but	finished
and	concluded	his	life	approaches	maid	in hysterics	crying
found	Pa's	belly	heaving	and	Dr Ewe	is helping	found
him	burst	sagging	badly	we	then	found	him
utterly	skinny	said he	I	have	spoke	with	the
dead	George	but he	know	not	the	coffin	maker
This	therefore	was	after	decided	following	such	messages as
He	sent	from	function	on	pleasant	height	of heaven.

TEN

BREAKFAST PICNIC

It is a constant source of astonishment to me that so many people want to live in towns. I never wanted to, and even at quite an early age would 'girn' a bit from time to time at my forced urbanisation. 'None of us *want* to live in town,' Elspeth would explain, patiently. 'We'd all much rather live in the country. We would live there if it were possible—but Daddy's patients all live in Knearsley, so we have to live here to be with them. Perhaps you'll be able to live in the country after you've grown up.'

But being grown up was a long time away, and meanwhile we took ourselves off to the country whenever we could manage it.

'The country' for us was the Yorkshire Dales, which we could reach in about an hour's driving, and many a pleasant afternoon did we spend in that lovely area. At first the road lay through a series of mill-oriented villages like Knearsley and Roddingly, with their stone houses and sooty little gardens, recreation grounds and blackish battlemented churches. Then—the first breakthrough—came the village of Burley-in-Wharfedale. Here the houses were of stone too, but they were older—eighteenth rather than nineteenth century—and their long straight gardens had old, gnarled trees in them, apples, and plums, giving a memory of more gracious times. One house had a big pear tree trained flat against its gable-end, and I always kept a special look-out for it when we passed it in its flowering time. It was mid April before the buds opened, as far north as that, and as it stood, arms wide, pressed back against the house wall, it always looked to me as bravely defiant as a Joan of Arc. This part of Yorkshire is not a country of lush flowerings and lavish blooms, but a cold, hard, late uppish area where things flower singly and with difficulty. The pear tree seemed to brace its cramped and knotted branches so steadfastly against the stone, and to bring forth with such pain and triumph its creamy cups of bloom. I suppose to me it was a symbol of what I was proud of in Yorkshire—the dogged, unflinching endurance, the unyielding pride that the harsh climate and terrain had instilled into its people.

After Burley, the landscape changed rapidly. A ridge of Millstone grit on the left developed into Ilkley Moor and on the right the limpid reaches of the Wharfe ran, sparkling, through broad green river-meadows studded with sheep and cattle.

We always seemed to go through Burnsall wherever we were heading, and Elspeth, looking at its exquisite Georgian rectory would always say 'Papa was nearly vicar here—he was offered the living, but he chose Boland instead.' Sometimes she used to say it in other places too, and we eventually developed a fiction that bishops and landowners from all over the dales had spent long and fruitless years hastening to lay their livings at Papa's feet. 'There's the turning to Hubberholme,' she might say. 'There's supposed to be rather a nice little church there...' 'And I suppose Papa was once nearly vicar of it, only he chose Boland instead?' one of us would chip in, with gentle mockery.

We had several favourite haunts for picnics when we were very little; Barden Towers, Bolton Abbey, and places like that, where we could eat our tea in green seclusion and have a prolonged play in the river. The smell of a clear-running, weed-streaming, fresh water river brings those days back with poignant vividness. Those little half-moon beaches of coarse white sand, those smooth, water-rounded stones, often so treacherously slippery and the roundly moulded cornices of white limestone were lapped so sweetly by the dark, clear, ever-travelling waters of the river; and there we paddled, played pooh-sticks, or made and sailed little boats of leaf and twig until it was time to go home.

Often we picnicked on the shores of Lake Semmerwater, and Thomas would tell us the legend: an old and weary traveller went through the little lakeside village one evening, knocking on every door and asking for shelter for the night. One and all turned him brusquely away until, limping and footsore, he turned from the village and slowly mounted the zig-zag road up the fell. At the top of the rise one cottage stood by itself, the home of an old shepherd and his wife; and when they saw the

114

old fellow toiling up the hill, they felt so sorry for him that they fetched him in and sat him down by the fireside before he even had time to ask. They set food before him—poor, but the best they had—green cheese and oatcake, and a generous slice off the side of bacon hanging from the rafters; and the wife boiled up a kettle, and with her own hands bathed his poor old calloused, buniony feet. Then they packed him off to sleep in their own bed, while they made do with the straw in the other end of the loft 'For,' they said, 'we see you have come from far, Father, and a long road lies ahead of ye tomorrow.'

But in the morning all was changed, for when the first light of dawn struggled through the tiny windows there arose from the bed not the wayworn traveller of the night before, but a young man, beautiful and terrible, who shone in that shadowy place with his own radiance. The old people were terrified, and cowered on the ground, but the young man spoke to them, and even his voice was full of power. 'Be not afraid,' he said. 'I am not what I seem, but I mean you no harm. I am an angel sent by our Heavenly Father to make trial of the people of this village, and sore have they failed, in the hardness of their hearts. For was it not written: "In as much as ye have done it unto the least of these, ye have done it unto Me." And for this rejection, the people of this village must pay, even unto the end of the world.' With this, the angel moved to the door and stood looking over the village that lay in the valley with the little tarn, hardly bigger than a pond, lapping its reedy banks beside it. He stretched out his hand, and somehow—they knew not by what means—all was changed. With a grumbling roar the waters rose, like a cauldron that boils over, and before their very eyes the village was engulfed. It was so sudden that there was no chance of escape for the sleeping villagers, and there they all lay, drowned in their beds while the flotsam and wreckage floated over their heads and the surging waters rocked the bell in the church steeple ding-dong, ding-dong, a flat and muffled chime.

The angel dropped his hands. 'So perish all who love not the Lord', he said, and then he faded from their sight, and they were left clutching each other's hands and staring at the water which now lapped the stone road only thirty yards below their cottage door . . .

We loved this story and had to hear it afresh every time we visited the great, ruffling lake. But we thought of it only as a legend, and it came as the greatest surprise to me when some archaeologists discovered quite recently, at a time of exceptionally low water, that there actually was a village down there after all. It was a bronze age fort, built on an island in the middle of the lake, and reached by a causeway, and the most fascinating thing that their researches revealed was that it had had to be evacuated in a hurry because a sudden rise in the lake level had inundated it.

But this fascinating coda to the story was still hidden in the womb of time when we used to visit Semmerwater, and we loved it not only for the story but because we could swim there, changing modestly into our bathing costumes behind a big oddly-shaped rock that was always known to us as 'the bear with no botty on', and listening, ever hopefully even as we splashed, for the forlorn note of the muffled, water-swayed bell.

Most of our picnics took place at what I take to be the conventional time for such junketings—the afternoon; but once we went on a breakfast picnic, which was so beautiful that I have remembered it all my life.

Nurse was still with us, so I must have been six or seven; and from the pictures that flash into my mind of the light, the birds, and the flowers, it must have been late May or early June. We were up at first light and away, racketing clonk-clonk-clonk-clonk over the dangerous wooden canal-bridge in Roddingley and through Woodley, Keigham and Yardon before they had sounded their six-o'clock hooters or blinked the sleep out of their eyes. By seven we were in the dales, and the rising sun reflected silvery from the overhanging bluff of Kilnsey Crag, whose feet are ever washed by the little stream that Tom yearned towards as he trudged after his master Grimes, before he was transformed into a water baby. On and on we drove, further in and higher up, and the low limestone walls lay along the edges of the lanes like looped pearls in the sunlight. Finally we abandoned the car, and set out to walk the last mile on foot, while the birds sang, and the rabbits popped into their holes at our approach, and the low sun stretched our shadows out long behind us.

There were sheep everywhere, blackfaces and swaledales, with

116

lambs at foot that glanced, terrified, out of black-masked amber eyes before racing away, or, more defiantly, stamped their tiny, shell-like hooves on the dew-silver grass and stood their ground. The turf, close-cropped, was resilient and springy beneath our feet, and a shower of song fell from the myriad larks in the air and rose from the blackbirds singing in the flowering hawthorns. It was like the morning of the world—like Paradise before the Fall—but a cool northern paradise, sparkling and fresh, with no serpent hiding in the wings. Over the bare, rounded hills, curlews bubbled and lapwings bleated their querulous alarms; and once a pair of ravens, with quiet, deep-voiced 'kronks' flapped over, stunting and sideslipping as they flew for very joy of their flight and the morning.

We were making for a place called Cowside Beck, a particular bit of it where we had picnicked before, and where the headlong little stream had gouged out a pool deep enough and long enough to bathe in. There was a good beach of pebbles too, rounded, smooth silvery ones, and here we made our fire. There was no shortage of wood. The beck, in its winter spate, had carried down plenty of rubbish—broken fencing-posts, dead reeds, branches, even a small hawthorn bush—and these lay, dead, dry, and white as picked bones, in a sort of tide-mark just where the pebbles met the grass. A few yards from the beck the remains of an old hedge offered us another source of fuel, as much as we liked to pick up. It had long ceased to be a hedge in the functional sense of the word, and had in fact degenerated into a gappy row of little trees, hazel, sloe and hawthorn, whose gnarled trunks and sparse twigs were all bent over in one direction by the prevailing wind. Tumbled stones covered in moss lay round their roots, the ruins of a fence once sheep-proof, long ago; dog-violets and prim-roses, blooming late in those high places, peeped out in charming profusion among the lichened roots and here and there were cowslips, not in the hedge, but springing, short-stemmed, straight from the sheep-nibbled turf. Dead boughs lay everywhere, ripped off by the gales of winter, and it was no labour to light a fire and bring it to the red-ember stage which is the best for cooking.

The air of the dales is like champagne—or rather better than champagne, purer, more sparkling and more stimulating, es-pecially at eight o'clock on a merry May morning; and the breakfast that Elspeth cooked over that open fire would have made a king weep with envy, if he could have had an appetite like ours.

There was porridge first of all—good salty porridge, because of her being an Irishwoman—a great big saucepanful, tasting of woodsmoke, and with the black marks on the underneath of the pan where the flames had leaped up and licked it. And then there were steaks, great big juicy bloody-middled beef-steaks, sizzled in butter and garnished with nothing but the brown, savoury drip from the frying pan, which we mopped up eagerly with bread at the end. I suppose we drank tea, but I don't remember. It is the fine solid, belly-filling, taste-bud-wooing steak and porridge that I remember, and the gentle flavour of sweet wood-smoke that permeated the whole, lifting it out of the run of ordinary eating and hallowing it forever in my memory. It was the sort of breakfast that Robin Hood might have eaten, with Little John and Will Scarlet down in the forest; or one of the heroes of the ballads about whom we read in our school poetry books—Johnny Armstrong, perhaps, or Young Lochinvar. It was a heroic breakfast.

After we had eaten, we boiled up a kettleful of water and washed up; and then we wandered around looking at the cowslips while the wagtails hopped up and cautiously tasted the scraps of porridge where the scourings of the pan had been emptied onto the grass.

When the statutory hour for digestion was over, we bathed. Our pool was a long, narrow cleft in the limestone, fed by a little waterfall at the top, and trickled out over round stones at the bottom into what you might call an arpeggio section of shallow, hurrying rapids. It was not very big; twenty strokes of even my feeble backstroke took you from one end to the other; but it was quite deep, and we all swam to and fro for a while, taking it in turns to stand under the little waterfall, and clinging to the slippery rocks for a rest in the deepest part where your feet could not find the bottom.

All picnics must end, and presumably we packed up our gear and drove home at some time during the day; but I have for-gotten all the threads that brought us back to the everyday world. Instead, my memory leaves us there, the fire still burning on the

118

pebbles, and us swimming in the deep clear pool, while the sun climbs over the green shoulder of the hill and the yellow cowslips in the short grass nod in the breeze, under the fluttering shadows of the stunted nut-trees.

ELEVEN

PRACTICAL JOKES

One of the luckiest dispensations of providence for us as a family was that we all had the same kind of sense of humour. 'Childish', 'stupid', 'infantile' snapped sour headmistresses at things I thought particularly funny, but I knew inside myself that the family would not only have laughed, but would have sent the joke forward improved and embellished by the mutually stimulating power of their comic invention.

Our jokes were not of the banana-skin school. Indeed, sometimes they existed in our own minds rather than in the world of reality. Like the time when Thomas's eye happened to be caught by an address of such superlative banality on an envelope somewhere that he couldn't help memorising it. 'I wish I had someone to write to who lived at such a collector's address as that,' he said wistfully. 'Why not?' we said, and by the time we had finished we had all written to them—or, rather, sent them Christmas cards. We sent them from such fictitious characters as 'Harry, Nettie and the children' and 'Colonel and Mrs Archie MacMurdo', and we sent them, with covering notes to friends and relations in all parts of the island—indeed, of the globe—to be posted so that they should arrive with a good selection of postmarks. The MacMurdos wrote from New England; Harry and Nettie, I seem to remember, lived in Newcastle-upon-Tyne. Of course, we weren't there when the cards arrived, but we got a good deal of simple pleasure out of imagining the head-scratchings and puzzlings of the recipients as the warm tide of greeting rose higher and higher in their desirable residences. We invented the things they would say to one another, endowing them with rich Yorkshire accents although in fact they lived somewhere in the south—and they, presumably, eventually resigned themselves to their unexpected popularity and found places on their shelves and mantelpieces for about thirty more cards than they had any right to expect.

Our own mantelpieces were always groaning with cards particularly after Papa came to live with us. Papa was a man of great charm, and the people he met never seemed to forget him. Throughout the year he conducted an extensive correspondence in his neat, tiny, sloping handwriting, and at Christmas all these friends and many more sent him cards. Old parishioners, golfing acquaintances, chance-met people on holidays, distant relations and family connections—all sent him cards, and the dusting took four times as long as it should throughout the weeks surrounding Christmas.

Many of these cards were of the sort that have the sender's name printed rather than written, and one year after I was married, Richard, as a mild joke, abstracted all these and sent them one by one to Desmond and me, which considerably swelled our meagre display. We, of course, were in no doubt about the origin of this particular bounty, and I carefully saved the cards in an envelope so that in the following December they could be posted off, one by one, back to Richard. Papa was the one who was puzzled when seeing a card sticking out of an envelope addressed to Richard, he glanced at it and saw that it had apparently been sent by his own old friends Colonel and Mrs Blazer whom he had met out in Singapore. 'How dooz Blazer come to know Richard?' enquired the card in Richard's distinctive writing when it arrived on our mat for the second time a year later.

We might have continued shuttling Papa's cards to and fro indefinitely, but we didn't, because by the time it was our turn to post them again in the December of the fourth year, we were under a cloud, and postal jokes were definitely out for the time being. The trouble was that we had started a stone that had turned into an avalanche, and once an avalanche is on its way there are very few who have the power to call it back. It was the magazine *Family Doctor* that was our downfall. Somehow a copy of it had fallen into our hands, and when we had read it we saw that it offered a service which seemed just the thing for a spot of mild waggery. A double page was divided into little boxes, and each box was the property of one of the firms advertising in that issue of the magazine. You wrote your name in the boxes of those manufacturers whose products you wanted to know more about, and sent the whole thing to the editorial offices of the magazine. We thought Richard might appreciate a bit more weight in his daily post bag, so with no small labour we wrote his name and address out fifty times or so, filled every box, and exposed him to a rush of pamphlets on everything from bridal lace to sanitary glazeware. At that time he was working as a solicitor in Derby and coming home to Knearsley for the weekends. So in order to spread the load we filled in some boxes for one address, and some for the other. Then we posted off the form, rubbed our hands, and settled back to await the rueful laughter that we were sure would shortly be forthcoming. But it was not. At first there was nothing, and then, after about a fortnight, we had a letter from my mother. At the end of it was a postscript which said 'I don't know what you and Desmond think you are doing sending all this stuff to Richard, anyway, please stop it. It's very silly and tiresome and not at all funny.' But of course, it was too late by now; we couldn't stop it. And worse was to come. We had accidentally copied his address in Derby wrongly, and the postmen who toiled up the hill to the wrong house with the myriads of leaflets and samples only to have to take them back and re-deliver them, were not amused. Nor was the occupant of the house we had inadvertently directed them to. Nor was the post office, who had to keep a girl at their Derby main office employed more or less full time for several weeks re-addressing Richard's mail. Actually they got quite disagreeable about it and started sending him terse notes suggesting that he inform his many correspondents of his *true* address. It was all very unfortunate.

The climax came when East Gate began to be besieged by an army of representatives all wishing to show Mr Richard Horner the very latest thing in self-seal baby pants or reliable rot-proof garage door hinges. Elspeth wrote again really angrily: 'Most of these representatives are local men, one or two of them have even been patients, and it's not very amusing to have to tell them, when they come to the door—thinking that it's at our request—that it's all a stupid practical joke.'

We were extremely penitent, but there was absolutely nothing we could do to stop it, and the whole business just had to die a natural death. But it put us off postal jokes for all time.

When Thomas was a medical student he too was a party to a

joke that misfired, though not with such a prolonged rumble as ours. He and his friends spent a merry afternoon sending off requests for brochures in other friends' names, choosing always the most ludicrously inappropriate goods for the individual concerned; and for one G. Smith they arranged a pamphlet describing a cunningly fashioned new kind of truss. He, of course was only about twenty-two years old, strong, tall and athletic, and innocent of any suspicion of a rupture. But his father, a choleric colonel, was ruptured and by an unfortunate turn of fate he shared his son's initial. So when the brochure arrived he picked it up, thinking it was addressed to him, and opened it. His roars of rage when he saw what it was shook the pictures off the walls and brought lumps of plaster crashing from the ceiling. 'Christ all bloody mighty!' he shouted, thumping the breakfast table with his fist until the cups danced in their saucers, 'is there no bloody privacy left? How the ----- do these ---s know about my bloody rupture?' He wrote a fire-breathing letter to the truss manufacturers but never managed to track down the true culprits, luckily for them.

Richard arranged an elaborate joke one summer day that was intended for me, but unbeknown to him, I suddenly decided to go to Leeds and took myself off; and the one who fell into the pit that he had so painstakingly dug was Papa. Richard was quite deft with wireless and things, having been a 'W.op. Tele.op.' during his national service, and he fixed things up in such a way that he could sit in his bedroom and speak into a microphone that was connected to the wireless in the drawing room. It was the summer of 1949 when the West Indian cricket touring team was making mincemeat of the M.C.C., with batting that stayed solid down to number 9 at least, and above all with the two unplayable spin bowlers, Ramadhin and Valentine. Richard, having laid his cunning snares without being seen by anyone, left the wireless on and the drawing room door open and retired to his bedroom to put the sad condition of English cricket right, for anyone at least who would believe it. Papa wandered into the drawing room and sat down, listening at first idly, to the commentary.

'And he's walking back to his mark. Only a short run. And he turns. And he's running up—Ramadhin, from the nursery end and—by jove, he's fairly cracked that through the covers for four! It's not often you see a batsman jump down the pitch to Ramadhin like that! So that's four more to Washbrook, a lovely stroke. And Ramadhin runs up again—a slower one this time—and he's hit him for SIX! Lofted over the square leg boundary! High over square leg's head! And this is a remarkable over! And he comes in to bowl—he bowls—AND HE'S HIT HIM FOR SIX AGAIN! This is phenomenal! This is making cricket history!—AND HE'S HIT HIM FOR SIX AGAIN!——'

At this point Elspeth came in and, recognising Richard's voice, she moved over to the wireless and went to switch it off, saying, 'You don't want to listen to this nonsense, do you, Papa?' But Papa, who was by now sitting on the edge of his chair with his eyes falling out of his head with excitement, cried out dramatically 'No, No! Don't switch it off, child! It's a phenomenon! He says it's making cricket history!' He was very nice about it when he realised that he had been sent up, particularly as it hadn't been meant for him at all. But Papa was nice about most things.

The most elaborate joke we ever indulged in developed purely by chance when the usual large family party had gathered at East Gate to celebrate Christmas. Someone had dug up from some deep cupboard an old set of 'teach yourself French' records, and we played them to our frivolous relations because they sounded so funny. They started with all the French vowel sounds in doublets, so to speak, each one said twice, once long and once short, with a curious emphatic sharpness: 'A! Aaaaa! O! Ooooo! Eu! Euuuu! E! Eeeee!' and so on—and then they proceeded to some nouns which they mouthed with the most exaggerated precision, rendering them almost di-syllabic with their emphasis on the final e. 'La mè-re! Le pè-re! Et . . . le bé-bé!' they spat in the tone of a High Anglican bishop who has been asked to say grace for an orgy. We liked it, and we thought around in case we could bring to mind the name of anyone else with whom we could share this bounty.

I have described the disposition of our road, whose left side was lined along its whole length with large stone houses, standing in gardens of anything from one to five acres, and at that time still nearly all in private occupation. Near the top of the road lived a family called Mason who were among our oldest friends. The father was the managing director of a large manufacturing concern in the neighbourhood, and I never remember a time when we were not on friendly terms, and visiting frequently at one another's houses. Like us, the Masons had three children, but they were the other way round from us—two boys and a girl—and they were a few years older than us, being young grown-ups when we were still children. Of the eldest brother, Michael, we were somewhat in awe, for he was up at Cambridge, and seemed a very great man in our eyes. The younger brother, David, we knew much better, and we liked and admired him very much, for he always provided some little entertainment for us whenever we went to tea. Sometimes it was conjuring, sometimes a magic lantern, sometimes a Punch and Judy show—once, even, a display of hypnotism, in which he displayed remarkable powers.

But the one we knew the best and loved the most was the daughter, whose name was Dinah. I suppose she must have been about eighteen at the time I first remember her, and in my eyes she always seemed absolutely perfect, haloed, as it were, in a cloud of golden light of the sort that is reputed to surround the immortals. She was tall and very good-looking and her hair was long, thick and golden, like the goose-girl's, which seemed very wonderful to us as we were all dark. She was elegant too, and wore lovely clothes, and rode well, and had a little car of her own in which she used to take us out sometimes for rides in the country. When I was grown up of course I got to know her as a real, much-valued human being, but when I reach back into my earliest memories it is as a goddess that I always see her—a bountiful, kind goddess.

In the years following the war it became habitual for us to invite the Masons to dinner at our house on Christmas Day, and for them to invite us back for another Christmas dinner at their house on Boxing Day. And so, it being Boxing Day when we started playing about with the French records, their name sprang naturally to mind when we were trying to think of someone else to play them to.

We rang them up and held the portable loudspeaker up to the

mouthpiece of the telephone while someone stood ready to lower the needle at the appropriate moment. David picked up the receiver. 'Knearsley 32591', he said briskly, 'David Mason speaking.' At a nod from the man at the telephone the needle was let down and the gramophone began to utter the noises. 'A! Aaaaa!' it said sternly. 'O! Ooooo! Eu! Euuuu!' David was non-plussed. 'Press button A,' he advised. 'We seem to have a very bad line. I can't hear what you're saying.' 'Ee! Eeeee!' replied the gramophone severely. 'La mè-re! Le pè-re! Et . . . . le bé-bé!' David's voice hardened. 'I don't know who you are or what you want,' he said. 'But you sound drunk to me. I should think you'd better go home and sleep it off!' Whereupon he hung up.

This was better than anything we could have expected, and, feeling our way cautiously, we pushed the joke along. Twice more during the day we rang up, desisting only when the goaded David said 'I've had quite enough of this sort of language, and if it happens again I'm going to call the police.' But by then the council of parents, uncles, aunts and cousins had put their heads together, and the shape of the rest of the joke was becoming apparent.

The Masons were bursting with news when we arrived up at their house for the dinner party that evening, and David made haste to tell us all about it. 'We've been having threatening telephone calls all day from some frightful drunk,' he said. 'I can't think who it can be. I can't understand a word he says, but it's obviously something very abusive.' 'How *awful*', we said. 'I wonder who it can possibly be? and many ideas were canvassed over the turkey and plum pudding and the fruit salad and Dinah's delicious home-made ice cream.

The subject had lapsed by the time dinner was over, and we all went into the long, beautiful, brilliantly-lighted drawing room to have coffee and surreptitiously slacken our tight sashes. We were a large party—twenty at least—and it was at this stage that Uncle Jim was able to creep away without his absence being noticed, and nip back down the road to East Gate. While we were drinking our coffee, the telephone rang again. David started to his feet. 'I'd better go,' he said to his mother, 'in case it's that chap again.' In a moment he popped his head round the door. 'It is!' he whispered, his face alight with excitement. 'It's him again! Come and have a listen, and see if any of you can make head or tail of what he's on about!'

So we all trooped out into the hall, and all took turns with the receiver while Jim obligingly kept the record going and David, tense as a bowstring, fairly hopped around in the background.

You could see why he was puzzled once you got the receiver to your ear, and you could see why he had found the visitation somewhat alarming. For the crisply enunciated details of French family life degenerated over the telephone into a low, menacing rumble in which no word could be distinguished but of whose aggressive intention there could surely be no doubt.

When Jim had hung up, we drifted back into the drawing room, busily discussing what we had heard. We had intended at this stage to break the joke and tell the Masons our guilty secret, but Jim, in a last burst of inspired improvisation, managed to bring the thing to a much better climax than any mere confession, and luckily he did it in time. As he was leaving East Gate again to rejoin the party (where his absence had still not been noticed), his eye fell upon the old portable wind-up gramophone that was once provided for the entertainment of the maids and, slinging it in the car with the record, he brought it up and set it to go in the Mason's hall, immediately outside the drawing room door. This was not part of the original plan, and we all jumped as we heard the well-known voice, restored now to its pristine clarity, enunciating its doubled vowels a mere few feet away from our chairs. 'Aaaaa, A!' it insisted. 'Ooooo, O! Euuuu, Eu!' David nearly hit the ceiling. 'How the hell did he get in here?' he shrieked and flung open the door—to be confronted by Jim, who with streaming eyes clung weakly to the door jamb, and the small black gramophone which sat squarely in the middle of the carpet reiterating still 'La mè-re! Le pè-re! Et . . . le bé-bé!'

TWELVE

MEALS AND CONVERSATION

We had tea at about five o'clock at East Gate in the drawing room, and afterwards everybody separated to do something or other till dinner time. Thomas and Elspeth usually had evening surgeries which lasted from six till eight; Richard and Gillian, who were both at university during the years I am thinking of, would go to their rooms and work; and somebody would cook the dinner. Sometimes it was me, and then, inevitably, it would be late. I had a fatal addiction to reading and even if I was firm with myself in the first instance and refrained from taking my current book into the kitchen with me ('Hev you seen *That Book*, choild?'), it was a hundred pounds to a pinch of snuff that my eye would be caught by some piece of print—the recipe book I was looking up canary pudding in, or last Tuesday's *Yorkshire Post* spread out on the newly-scrubbed table under the window—and then one thing would lead to another and Elspeth would come in at eight and find me bottom up, elbows on the table, oblivious to the passage of time and with the canary pudding still chirping in its basin . . .

Another characteristic of my food was that it tended to be herby. When I was seventeen I bought a cookery book by one Peter Pirbright called *Off the Beeton Track* which inspired me to all sorts of experiments, and I account it one of the most gracious manifestations of good manners of my family that they ate up my productions with a most convincing appearance of appreciation. It was not for years afterwards that I realised Thomas, for instance, really doesn't like herbs in cooking at all . . .

Not only did he conceal this, but he further gave rein to my enthusiasm by planting a whole lot of different herbs in rows in a bed in the side garden where, under his green-fingered touch, they flourished exceedingly. There were lots of different kinds. Some, like wormwood and rue, we never used, but there was basil too, and tarragon, and lovage, and marjoram, and thyme, and fennel—even borage, with blue flowers to float in a cooling drink.

We always had a drink before dinner. Even on my cooking nights there would be ten minutes while the plates warmed up in the oven when we all went into the drawing room ('Take your apron off, Elizabeth') and had a glass of sherry together or something else if you didn't like sherry. Richard didn't like any alcoholic drink so he would usually mix up a pitcher of iced tomato juice carefully seasoned with salt, pepper, lemon juice and Worcester Sauce, served in a black antique jug with a pewter lid, a red handle, and pictures of Greek charioteers on the sides. There were three of those jugs, large, middle-sized and small, and I have them now. They remind me each time I look at them of those happy days at East Gate.

Elspeth cooked when she didn't have a surgery, and, being good at everything she undertakes, she used to serve food of unvarying perfection. It was simple food, but well bought and well cooked, and it has left me for ever imprinted with a basic preference for the superb plainness of the classic English cuisine over all the rich fancies of the Continent.

'Elizabeth,' she would say to me, pushing a punnet into my hands and spinning me deftly round so that I was facing the door instead of the evening paper spread out on the kitchen table, 'Would you go to the vegetable garden and pick some broad beans. And some parsley for the sauce. Oh, and a few sticks of rhubarb—nice ones!' So I would go. And it was a pure delight to be in our vegetable garden in the evening, with the westering sun turning the high sandstone walls to red-gold, and the columns of midges dancing under the elm trees, and the noise of the busy manufacturing day all hushed, with only a few swifts still screaming against the pure sky going slowly dim so far above. I would pick a basket of beans, bronze-green and pungent, heavy-podded in their ample rows, and tuck a fistful of tight-curled parsley down at one end of the punnet. Then I would go up to the rhubarb bed at one end of the garden and pull a few sticks, snapping the huge leaves off and leaving them wilting on the ground.

We had special rhubarb at East Gate and I only wish I could

get hold of some now. The area round Leeds and Bradford is famous for its rhubarb-growing and this stuff of ours was *crème de la crème*, being a strain that had won a lot of prizes in its day even in the fierce competition of such a district. It was a special strain of a variety called Dawkes' Champion, and the original root had been given to Thomas by a patient on condition that he never showed it or gave or sold a bit of the root to anyone. Over the years it had grown and flourished in our vegetable garden, and we now had a row about fifteen yards long running almost the full width of the plot tucked under the end wall. Each stalk was as thick as a child's arm and weighed about three quarters of a pound and the leaves were enormous, as big as elephants' ears. But in spite of the size, it was always sweet and snapping-tender, and it cooked to a lovely bright pink, perfect for a pie.

It was a pleasure to linger in the vegetable garden while the sun slowly sank behind the church tower on the other side of the road and the hens in their adjacent enclosure chivvied each other in to bed.

Among the vegetables were occasional rows of flowers, for Thomas often grew packets of lupins and delphiniums from seed, and these would be planted out in the vegetable garden for their first blooming so that only the best might be promoted to the august company of the long double herbaceous border at the bottom of the garden. It was agreeable to watch them develop and spot the winners as their buds gradually filled up and their petals unfolded.

'I had such a funny little boy in my Roddingley surgery this afternoon,' remarked Elspeth later as she stood at the side table in the dining room serving out the baked turbot, delicate as a kiss. 'I had to laugh (is that enough for you, Papa?). He was only about eight, and he had quite a nasty cut on his knee. I had to put three stitches in. And he was awfully good, I must say. He didn't cry or anything. But all the time I was putting them in he kept muttering away, and his mother kept shaking him and saying "Shoot oop!" and "Ee, I'm that ashamed of 'im, Doctor!" till I began to listen to what he was saying. And what it turned out to be was "Booger-booger-booger-booger-booger" under his breath, as fast as he could string it together. I had to laugh. Beans, Gillian? Tommy?'

As we settled to our turbot, our broad beans and new potatoes with a great sauce-boat full of fresh green parsley sauce, Thomas too had a tale to recount. 'I was in Blucher Street,' he said, 'and I'd got out of the car when a little girl came running along the pavement towards me shouting out "Tin Towers! Tin Towers!" I really didn't know what to reply. I was quite taken aback. Then I realised that she wasn't speaking to me at all, but to a group of children behind me, and that what she meant by "Tin Towers" was "It isn't ours!" '

'Could you all come out into the garden for half an hour after dinner?' asked Elspeth. 'I was noticing that there are an awful lot of raspberries to pick.' So when we had finished our rhubarb pie and cream and cleared away the plates we all sallied forth, armed with pudding basins, into the side garden, and waded among the wet leafy raspberry canes where the level rays of the sun struck fire from the drops of an earlier shower. Then we went back to the kitchen and while the boys washed up, the female element of the family weighed up the raspberries and made them into jam which was lined up in a beautiful square block of pots on the table under the window, waiting to be covered the next day. Fragrance of hot jam filled the kitchen and the kettle bubbled on the stove as Gillian made a big pot of tea and carried it into the drawing room in time for the nine o'clock news on the wireless.

It was always like that at East Gate. Jobs were shared, work was done decently and in order, and any little incident that happened to anybody during the day was saved up to be recounted at the next meal, when we were all together. Like the brief fantasy of Thomas and the Hat, for example. 'I was driving up New Road this morning,' he told us, 'when I saw a woman walking down the pavement wearing an absolutely enormous hat. It was quite a striking shape, too, really stylish, and I wondered for a second who she could be, to have enough courage to wear a thing like that in Knearsley. And then I got closer, and I saw that it wasn't a woman at all, it was a plumber, walking along the pavement balancing a lavatory on his head . . .'

On another evening while we all ate steak and kidney pie with fresh garden peas, Elspeth told us about another of her patients,

131

a boy of about twelve, who had come to her evening surgery with a moth in his ear. 'I had a look first, of course, with the auroscope, and when the light shone down his ear it reflected in this little pair of red eyes. It gave me quite a jump—there I was, suddenly, eye to eye at quite close range with this malevolent little face!' A quick syringing of the ear soon floated out the unwelcome visitor and as it lay, struggling feebly in the kidney dish, its late host looked at it with awe and observed admiringly 'By 'ec! It's feightin' yet!'

We were often sent into the garden for a mass effort at picking this and that after dinner, particularly during the sweat pea season. The sweet peas exercised over us a tyranny as unyielding as any dictator's, for they had to be picked about twice a week so that they would not stop flowering so that they could go on being picked about twice a week . . . and so on. We would all be provided with scissors and would spend a pleasant half-hour snipping away in the deep, slanting, honey-coloured light, and then we would gather up our armfuls of butterfly bounty and carry them into the house to be arranged. Every vase and vessel in the house would be pressed into service and there would be sweet peas everywhere. We usually divided them into related colours so that you might get one group of all blues, ranging from the delicate lavender of a summer morning to the deep sultry purple of a thundercloud; and another of exquisite pink picotees showing off against winged frilly blossoms of deepest cream. We had sweet peas in the hall, in the drawing room, on the landing, in the bedrooms—even in the surgery, and the whole house drowned in their fragrance.

On Sundays we always had a little tea-party. During the years I was growing up, food was rationed, and Elspeth's sister, Nora, who lived in Bruddersford, and her family were registered with us for eggs. We had their egg coupons with which we used to get meal to keep extra hens, and we provided them, in exchange, with a dozen or two eggs a week, depending on how well the hens were laying—which was far more than they would have got if they had taken their coupons to a grocer's shop in the ordinary way.

The family consisted of Nora, her husband George (who was a headmaster) and their daughter, our cousin, Hilary. Hilary was born during the war, and was consequently much the youngest of the party, but she always behaved herself very well and used to play very contentedly for hours with a pretty copper kettle which hung on a stand that had once had a spirit lamp as part of its equipment, in the dining room.

The ostensible purpose of the Ps' weekly visit was to collect their eggs, but we always enjoyed it as a social occasion, for they were witty and gay and there was always plenty to talk about. Sunday was technically a day off for Thomas and Elspeth, although every second week one of them had to be on duty for emergencies, and sometimes also they would arrange to do little operations like tonsillectomies or the removal of cysts on that day—in the patient's house, on the kitchen table, with one of them operating and the other anaesthetising. Usually, however, it was the one day of the week when we were all home together, and we thoroughly enjoyed it.

A modicum of housework had to be done ('Just dust the tops of everything, it looks so much better . . .'), but the bulk of the morning was devoted to cooking. I don't know how Elspeth managed it with rationing, but somehow she always seemed to have enough sugar and marge for a couple of cakes, and of course for us eggs were no problem.

She made the most lovely cakes. Being Irish, born and bred, she could always knock up a beautiful soda bread, and any milk that went sour in our house was always saved for this. Another of her specialities was chocolate cake which she always managed to cook moist, so that it sliced with a glisten on it, like a furrow in a ploughed field. She would often sandwich two of these dark, rich chocolate cakes together with butter cream powerfully flavoured with crème de menthe, and top the whole thing with a quarter of an inch of fudgy chocolate frosting. It was absolutely delicious, but so rich that one was only able to eat a very small slice at a time.

Another favourite cake was called 'Horner cake', being a particularly pleasant light fruit cake that had come down from that side of the family, and was always baked in a loaf tin. The recipe started 'Take . . . and beat for half an hour.' It is inconceivable to me that anyone could have done so, and I certainly never do—but then my Horner cake never tastes quite as good as

133

that which I remember from those distant days—perhaps that is why!

For our Sunday teas, as well as scones or soda bread and a couple of cakes, we would always make two or three different kinds of sandwiches. These were always very small and thin, with all the crusts cut off, and were served in lovely Sheffield plate entrée dishes which looked beautiful on the table. The sandwich fillings were always savoury—potted meat, egg, salmon, tomato, cress, cucumber, or even sometimes sandwich spread—and they were so delicious that there were never any left over.

Through most of the year we ate in the dining room, but when the weather was fine in the summer we often took our tea out into the garden, though this in no whit abated its formality. The big dining table of mahogany was too heavy to be carried out so a smaller one, a seventeenth-century oak gate-leg, would have to deputise. This table, polished until it looked like black water, would be spread with a cloth of lace or openwork (we had quite a selection) and set with all the paraphernalia of best china, silver teapot, hot water jug and cream jug, and lump sugar with silver tongs. We had special small napkins that were only used at tea time, and the loaded table looked quite beautiful under the glancing shadows of the high-overarched wych elm.

One of the pleasures of the Ps' visit was the detailed walk-round and inspection of the garden that always had to take place, for my Uncle George P. was a keen gardener like Thomas, and always wanted to see how everything was getting on. His own gardening was complicated by the fact that their house had been a kennels for many years before they bought it, and the garden was a foot deep in trampled dog-dirt before he began to dig it. Dog manure is one substance that even the most maniacal muck-and-mystery text books don't give you much guidance on, so we were always glad to hear of another successful braird of peas, or another flush of buds on the *Violinista Costa*.

Thomas used to buy large quantities of stable manure for our garden—a commodity not too difficult to come by in those days of petrol rationing and horse-drawn delivery carts. This was delivered in a tipping cart, and barrowed around as required, which led to a misunderstanding on Gillian's part when she was about four years old. A two-ton load had been dumped in the yard and the horse and cart that had brought it, having completed the tip, had moved forward a pace or two. Gillian, coming round the corner with Thomas saw the heap steaming gently in the frosty air and looked at the scene with amazement. 'Daddy', she whispered, full of respectful awe, 'Did that Horse do All That?'

THIRTEEN

RECREATION GROUND

The one and a half acres of garden in which our house stood was fairly evenly distributed around it. A head-high stone wall separated us from New Street; the twelve foot beech hedge ran across the bottom of the garden between us and the nursing home. At the back of the house another high wall bounded the yard and vegetable garden, backing onto the little gardens of Prospect Street; but down the long side of our garden where we most needed protection, we had hardly any. For our eastern neighbour was the recreation ground, and here the ground fell away a little, so that the boundary wall was only four feet in height from their side, and a mere foot or so on ours. It was indeed more of a retaining wall than a defence, with only the capstone course showing above ground level. A belt of tall trees ran down that side of the garden which effectively screened us and the 'reccers' from one another's view; but nothing that we could erect succeeded for long in keeping them at bay when apple time came round.

Scrumping is a vice to which mankind seems to have been incurably addicted ever since the days of Eden, and some memorable actions were fought over the years. Back in the 1920s, Thomas caught two little boys of about ten. Taking them into the yard, he said to one of them 'Bend over'. Then he put a small bamboo cane into the other one's hand, and said 'Now give him a whack.' Perhaps nervousness lent an unintentional vigour to the little boy's arm, or it may have been that he simply did not know his own strength. At any rate, he laid into his mate with such a right good will that when the latter came upright, he was what Chaucer would have called 'wood wrath', and, the rod of correction being put into his hand, he too meted out vengefully a very adequate punishment to his companion.

Another time the captured were two little girls and, deeming hitting inappropriate, Thomas took them to the vegetable garden and instructed them to do some weeding as reparation. Then he went on his afternoon round and totally forgot them. It was about six o'clock when a timid knock came on the back door, and two tired, bedraggled little girls stood there, meekly asking my mother 'Can we go home now, please, Mrs Horner, because there a'nt any weeds left?'

I once caught a tiddler, a little boy of five or six. I was about sixteen at the time—sufficiently senior to him to be awe-inspiring —so I growled at him a bit and then put him out of the street door with instructions to go straight home. I don't know what the other children in the recreation ground thought I'd done with him—eaten him, perhaps. At any rate, they all lined up along their side of the wall and there they stood, chanting 'You give that little lad back' for two or three hours, while I sat on a rug under the flowering cherry and read Spenser's *Epithalamion*.

What made these depredations particularly annoying for us was the fact that the children always took the apples long before they were any use, when they were about the size of billiard balls. It was as trophies that they wanted them, not as food. The best deterrent Thomas ever devised was a rickety-looking fence of very large-mesh wire netting, which he erected on fragile posts above the wall. The scrumpers rubbed their hands in anticipation when they saw this pathetic affair—but they were rubbing them in dead earnest a few moments later, after their first attempt to scale it. For Thomas had painted it all over with some very viscous, nasty, black, used sump oil, and now, lurking behind a bush, he listened in silent glee to the disgusted cries of 'Ee!', 'Flippin' 'ec!' and ''E's coovered it all wi' mooky stooff!'

The vandalism that plagues playgrounds nowadays was un-heard of then, and the worst that ever happened was that a child fell off a swing and hurt itself. I remember one or two knees brought round to the surgery to be stitched, and once, when somebody had knocked himself out falling off the roundabout the vicar's son arrived, breathless, at the back door calling out 'Doctor! Doctor! come quickly! There's a boy in the Rec. and he's senseless!'

In the evenings, when the younger elements had gone to bed the hobbledehoys gathered in the park, lounging on the swings and putting the world to rights or indulging in horseplay as the opportunity offered. When Thomas was working in that side of the garden he could overhear what they were saying, and often came in quoting vivid snatches of conversation.

'Margrit!' (for instance)

''Ellow!'

'Margrit! 'Ave yer got yer corsets on?'

'It's not necessary! Ah said, it's not necessary!'

Sounds of scuffling, followed by a great vulgar guffaw of laughter, and an adolescent's cracking voice raised in a triumphant shout 'She's soobmittin'!'

Once a group of three or four had fallen into a discussion of the problems of Israel and the Palestinian refugees. One young lad was in no doubt of the solution; 'It's easy!' he kept declaring 'Shoot t'bloody Jews! That's all y'ave to do. That'd settle it.' But one of the older ones turned on him and put him down with a sarcasm so ponderously silky that we all use his phrase to this day. 'There are people', he said, ''oo of bin discussing this problem for over thirty years. And then along cooms the *brainy* one—thirteen year old, or p'raps twelve—and solves it in a minute!' 'Along cooms the brainy one'—you know at once when somebody murmurs that, that you've been too clever by half again.

We had many other fruits besides apples in our garden, but they never seemed to tempt thieving children. We had gooseberries, lots of them, in a big bed in the side garden under a high, crumbling brick wall. If your heart was broken (as mine tended to be once a fortnight or so, being a fragile organ) it was a good place to go for a brood. Crouching on the hot earth, slightly scratched by the thorns one could press exploratorily on one's sorrow as one might test a bruise, and the bit in Keats' 'Ode to Melancholy' where the poet says

> Though seen of none save he whose strenuous tongue
> Can burst Joy's grape against his palate fine

is forever associated in my mind with gooseberries, red or yellow, sweet-fleshed, but with sour, hairy skins tasting slightly of soot . . .

We had lots of strawberries too, strawberries 'for cat and dog' as the Yorkshire saying goes. Yorkshire people have some curious dialect expressions. 'She's right bonny' means fat, not good-looking, and 'Ah'm getting a bit clever now' means recovering after being ill. If you are *not* feeling better, though, and the doctor asks how you are it is standard to say, 'Nay, Ah don't frame at all, Doctor. Ah feel like Barney's bull—boogered!' Coming back to our strawberries, we had several beds of them. Part of the Little Hill was a strawberry bed, and another was in the vegetable garden. Oddest of all was a long single row of plants in a narrow bed that divided the long herbaceous border from the lawn. Leaning back on the one-course stone edging, the berries ripened most beautifully, and a tunnel of wire netting kept the blackbirds at bay for that all-important strawberry month. There were several varieties here and there in the garden, but by far the most fragrant and luscious were the Royal Sovereigns, which for my vote have never yet been surpassed.

Having plenty of strawberries we used to get tired of them straight, with sugar and cream, and we made lots of other things with them for pudding. Strawberry shortcake was good, particularly any left over until the next day, but the favourite of all which we had as often as we could get it was strawberry pie. I was amazed when I grew up to discover that the world was full of people who didn't know that you *could* put strawberries in a pie. What the poor souls have been missing! For if I were granted just one helping of strawberries per annum I would not hesitate for a moment to have them in a pie rather than neat. It is a plate pie, ideally, with two crusts, and you use short crust pastry and just press the berries down lightly upon it, sprinkling them with sugar and being generous with the fruit, for it shrinks a good deal in cooking. When it is done, the top crust will be bumpy and the lower one juice-soaked here and there—and you will be tempted to eat it immediately. But it will pay you to let it go cold, or nearly—and then as a reward for your self-control, as your knife slips into the crumbling pastry, the aroma! the fragrance! It is ambrosial.

Raspberry pie is as good, which is saying something, and real bilberry pie, if you can get that most magical fruit, is an experience of extreme sensuousness. But I never seem to see the real bilberry now, and the frozen and tinned ones are travesties of

139

the true flavour. I imagine the thing is to pick them oneself and get two pleasures out of them, in picking and eating, in the same way as you get two good warms out of firewood you have chopped yourself.

FOURTEEN

KNEARSLEY

Before the industrial revolution, the West Riding of Yorkshire was a bonny, fertile agricultural country of rolling hills and clear salmon-breeding rivers. You can get a good idea of it by looking at Girtin's water-colour of Kirkstall Abbey 'bosomed high in tufted trees', with long, sheep-dotted pastures stretching down to the then limpid waters of the River Aire.

But by the time I was a child in Knearsley, in the 30s and 40s of this century, all this rural innocence had retreated to the status of a folk-memory. Most of the main part of the village, which rambled away down a steep hill at right angles to the main Leeds and Bradford road, was built in Victorian times when the big mills were founded with their mysterious processes and products that, as an outsider, you didn't understand. 'Tops & Noils', said the notice-board outside one black, cliff-like structure, throbbing with the hum of its huge machinery. 'Mungo & Shoddy', announced another. 'Fents & Pieces', 'Fells & Hides' or, more comprehensibly, 'Dyeing & Finishing', they towered over the village streets, and their strident buzzers imposed a most rigid discipline on the pale, grim-faced people who worked in them. Not as bad as it had been, though. One of Thomas's patients, on old man, told him once how he used to go to work with his father when he was twelve, with a four-mile walk to the mill and a starting hooter at six in the morning. 'And one day in t'winter I felt reight bad—'flu it wor, or summat a'sort. A thowt Ah'd fall over, it wor that bad. And Ah'd gone 'appen two mile, and Ah says to me Dad "Feyther", Ah says to 'im, "Ah'm bad, Ah can't go on." And 'e looks at me and 'e clouts me over t'ear and knocks me down. Then 'e picks me oop and clouts me ower t'other ear and knocks me down again. Then 'e picks me oop again and says "Can yer go on now?" And Ah says "Aye, Feyther" and Ah did, tha knaws!' A truly terrible story, but I fear probably a terribly true one.

But by the time I really got to know Knearsley, such dreadful days were long gone. The war, with its big demand for cloth for uniforms, brought prosperity for the woollen industry, and the mill people's full wage packets were reflected in a general rise in the economy of the whole place. All the shops seemed to do all right in spite of the wartime shortage of goods, and one popped in and out of them all down the High Street like a rabbit making use of a series of familiar burrows.

Not that I ever popped into the first shop in the street if I could avoid it, for the woman who owned it was embarrassingly fond of me. 'You're called Lizzy, loov, aren't yer?' she would crow at me—inaccurately, as it happened, for I was called Elizabeth or Libby, but never, never Lizzy—'And so am I! Two on us! Us Lizzies'll 'ave ter stick together, won't we, loov?' and so on and so forth, clasping me to her ample overalled bosom and rumpling my hair while I squirmed with distaste. 'The Lizzy woman' we called her, and often crossed the road to avoid going close to her door for she had been known to nip out and pet me, even more hideously, right there on the pavement. As she sold ice cream and was the only one to do so in the village, I was occasionally compelled to cross her threshold, but I only ever did so with a good shelter-belt of friends and relations around me, and got out again as soon as possible. She never made any attempt to cuddle any of the others, her unwelcome affection being reserved only for me.

There was no such problem at the next shop which was a sweet shop, smelling of sherbet and liquorice, with a long, bulls-eye-glassed window, and crates of lemonade bottles on their sides. Mrs L. was stout and kind and slow. She had a wart on the side of her pale, squashy nose, and wore long black flower-embroidered crêpe dresses like our grandmother; and she never minded how long you took to decide whether your penny should buy Spanish or toffee, or lucky dip, which was a little sugar box with a hard top and a charm in it, neatly wrapped in a motto; but her husband was different. He was sour and cross, with a nicotine-stained white moustache, and his small, ill-tempered eyes, as pale-lashed as a pig's, fairly snapped with resentment.

'Mek yer mind oop, can't yer!' he would shout, impatiently, almost before you had got the penny out of your pocket, and when you did choose he would push the sweets across the counter at you as pettishly as if you had offered to pay him in dried leaves. If we saw through the window that he was minding the shop we were inclined to go on and spend our pocket money somewhere else.

There was C's, the newsagents, for instance, which was a very nice shop. It was little and dark, with a strong smell of fresh newsprint but it wasn't the papers or comics that we liked there, but the toys. You could get lots of things for threepence there in those days—lead animals for farm and zoo, soldiers, cars, crayons, painting-books, marbles, whip-tops—and, most prized, small cardboard boxes which contained a small celluloid doll, a tin bath and a tiny cube of rubber sponge. These disintegrated while you looked at them but we loved them so much that we bought them week after week and the good Mr and Mrs C. would spread out their goods on the counter with the gravest courtesy, and assist in our choice as if the success of their business really depended on whether we went away with a doll and a bath or a blood alley.

If we had practised self-denial for a week or two and accumulated a shilling, there was another shop we would visit further down the street. This was a draper's shop, where amid the fragrance of new cotton we would pore over tray cloths ready printed for embroidery and choose hanks of bright silk for our laborious lazy-daisy stitch. Gillian was particularly choosy and insisted on picking out just exactly the right crinolined lady walking between just exactly the perfect hollyhocks, which usually entailed looking through the entire stock. This business was run by a Mrs H. and her husband had his own business as a carpenter. He used to work in a yard at the back of the shop and he often came in, in his long white apron, while we were there. It was Gillian who amused him. Many years later we found out that he used to say to his wife, 'Do come out and fetch me when that little Gillian Horner comes in. I do love to see her having a look at all the stock, all so serious, making her mind up. It's all that important to her! She does make me laugh!'

One hazard that you would be sure to encounter going down

our High Street was an old man known as Squire Reed. He had no squirearchical pretentions; he was simply christened Squire, just as Americans are sometimes christened Duke or Earl; and he was generally known as a bad lot. It was said that he had been a dog-thief, but he was too old for that sort of thing by the time I knew him, and he had degenerated instead into a permanent nuisance, a kind of one-man obstacle course that you had to get past in the best way you could. We could have dealt with him more easily if we had been able to cheek him, but the rule there was absolute: never, never, in any circumstances, might a child be rude to a grown-up. So we had to put up with his vagaries with the best grace we could muster, and he played on our good manners in return and made himself as objectionable as he possibly could.

You could see him most mornings, just before opening time, shambling his way down the High Street with his stick towards the Blue Boar, a mean public house which he frequented. If you passed him on the same pavement, he would shoot out his stick and make scooping lunges at your legs, so that you either had to jump over it like a skipping rope, or dart out of reach onto the road, smiling fixedly as if you really found it all a very good joke. If we saw him in time, we would cross to the other side, but you had to do it unobtrusively, for if he caught sight of your manoeuvre, he would stand on the edge of the pavement and shout after you, and neither delicacy nor the law of slander in any way hindered the free flow of his self-expression. One day in spring, when the first clement weather had tempted all the old men out of hibernation, Thomas overheard a fairly typical shouted exchange between the Squire and one of his cronies who was creeping up the other side of the street, bound for the Liberal Club.

'Why, yer gaumless owd booger!' cried the ancient. 'Arent-ta dee-ad yet?'

'Nay!' wheezed Squire. 'As long as Ah can eat and drink and piss and shite Ah shall noan dee!' With which they waved their sticks encouragingly at each other and parted on a creaking tide of senile cackles, the one uphill to the fusty warmth of the Liberal Club, the other down to the more relaxed delights of the Boar.

Children had to watch out for his stick, but to grown-ups Squire presented a different hazard. He was a button-holer. If he could once get you to stop and talk to him, it was difficult to get away without actual rudeness, and his conversation was not of the wittiest. He was crabby as well as coarse, and there were wags who averred that with his interminable stories and cyanosed countenance, he must be the original 'Blue Bore' for whom the pub had been named. He had a tedious trick of mis-hearing what you said and galloping off in all directions on a misapprehension, in the course of which he usually took the opportunity of telling you something to your disadvantage. 'We were thinking of driving out to the Dales this afternoon', Thomas told him one day, 'and going for a walk up on the top, on the sheepwalk.'

'Seaport! Seaport? There's no seaport i' t'Yorkshire Dales, which Ah'd a' thowt you'd a' knawn, Doctor. You must be dafter than yer look, that's all I can say . . .' and so on and so on, punctuated by vehement shakings of his victim's lapel, and the regular splashing of his nose-drop onto the pavement, or the toe of your boot.

If you had crossed the road to get away from the Squire, you might drop into the butcher's shop for a pork pie or indeed simply to pass the time of day. For the butcher's family were all charming. They were great big people, tall, stout and black-haired, who never addressed anyone except in a Force Nine shout, and they were always frantically busy. Hither and thither they flashed, knives or cleavers in hand, chopping, slicing, sharpening, wrapping, but maintaining their conversation in a series of stentorian witticisms flung at you as they passed in the broadest of broad Yorkshire. Only one of the family was still slight, and that was the youngest, a girl. At the age of nine she was still a mere sliver of a child but pretty as could be with her short-cut dark hair, dark eyes, and gamin features. 'Ah wor oop at t'football club New Year's Day', she told Elspeth once, with an irresistible giggle, 'And I 'ad me trousers on, and me balaclava, and they thowt Ah wor a lad, so they let me go into t'changin' room! Eee! Mrs Horner! You should a' seen it! Talk about bare booms!'

On another occasion she was to have her tonsils out and she

said, very seriously, 'And me Mam said special Ah wor to ask you to cut me sweerin' string at t'same time!'

The butcher himself was a compulsively active man. Indeed, one time when he had lumbago and was condemned to bed-rest, Elspeth, calling to visit him, was surprised to find him not there. 'Is that you, Doctor, loov?' called his wife from the shop. 'Nay, it's no good lookin' there. 'E said 'e couldn't stand it no more so 'e got downstairs slow, like, on 'is backside, and 'es i' t'garage, tekkin' t'car to pieces.' And there he was, sitting on the floor surrounded by oily bits and pieces looking as guilty as a cat in a pantry. 'Nay, loove, don't mek me go back oop there!' he bellowed, piteously. 'Ah can't stand it. It's wuss nor prison to me, joost to lie there doing nowt!'

On the same side as the butcher, but further down the hill, lived the redoubtable Mrs G. Her house opened flat onto the pavement, and in all but the coldest weather she was there all the time in the open doorway, like a sea-anemone waiting with tentacles agape for the scraps of excitement or entertainment that the street could bring her. She was a tall woman with stringy grey hair in a tight bun, and a pair of clear-rimmed spectacles, and she hung over the street like a kind of one-woman Greek chorus, enquiring, admonishing or commenting in her strident voice—a sort of perpetual third person to the action of the village.

'Ello love! Back from school, are yer?' she would cry like a peacock foretelling rain, when she saw me walk down the road on my vacations from the university. ' 'Ow are yer gettin' on wi' yer lessons? You 'aven't got a man yet, Ah see, loov, 'ave yer? Never mind—keep on trying—it's dogged as does it . . .' and so on, to my great embarrassment. Thomas and Elspeth got it even worse. 'When you have to visit her near Christmas time', explained Thomas, 'she's so hospitable she insists that you have a bit of her Christmas cake. And I must say it always looks very nice. But she's got a dreadful way of blowing her nose on her apron—and then she picks it up and gives the knife a good rub with it as she goes to cut the cake—it fairly makes my stomach heave. Actually I must admit I've told her I'm not allowed to eat Christmas cake—I'd be sick if I had to, I really think . . .'
'Funnily enough I've told her exactly the same thing!' laughed

146

Elspeth. 'She must think we're a proper family of weaklings!'
'Better that than have to eat it!' responded Thomas.

The relativity of size is a thing that often makes me smile. I live now near a town that I'm proud of, which is very important indeed. It is a county town, with the police headquarters, the County Hall, the big main hospital, the central Fire Service, and everything handsome about it—and it boasts 13,000 inhabitants. Knearsley in the 30s was a tiny place just a short step up from a hamlet, and so small that it came to be considered too small to be a viable administrative unit and was swallowed by its larger neighbour, Poddingley. And yet even then it had a population of 10,000. 'Ah well, it's all according,' as Nurse was wont to say.

It was very much a village even after it had been swallowed, and kept for a long time its symbols of independence. These lived in two glass-doored sheds fronting on to the High Street and we had to stop and admire them whenever we passed that way on our daily walk with Nurse. One was the fire-engine, Charlie, and the other was Sarah, a steam-roller.

Charlie was lovely, vermilion, gleaming, with brass cleaned to whiteness and a bell in his brow. Sarah—a Fowler if my memory does not fail me—was also full of brasswork but her paint was dark green. They were much loved and cherished and their names were inscribed over their stable doors, so that everyone knew what they were.

Looking at Charlie and Sarah, and admiring the firemen's helmets, brass-crested, on their pegs all round the walls, was a ritual stop on a walk down the High Street. And just after the Charlie-Hof was another, for if you turned aside, down a little unmade road, you could get to a bridge that ran over a stream— and the stream was bright blue. It must have come from a dye-works and with hindsight I see it as something disgusting with its clouds of steam, its slimy grey banks, and its smell like a big laundry-copper; but then we thought it was charming and would always step out of our way to admire it as it prattled along its polluted way with a mottling of pale grey suds on its azure breast . . .

After Charlie and the stream came a kind of no man's land with a pub or two and a mill, and the entries to several courtyards of the lowest kind in the district—the nearest approach to slums

147

you could find in Knearsley. They were the oldest of the industrial revolution houses in the village and they tucked themselves into its corners in the most haphazard way, without any attempt at regularity or organisation. Some of them were clustered round yards where a few animals were kept in makeshift sheds; many of them were back-to-backs, approached up unmade roads crisscrossed all the way by washing-lines. All of them used batches of communal lavatories at the street-ends, and none of them had a garden or much accommodation of any sort. Two up and two down was the usual pattern, with one cold tap in the scullery if you were lucky, the stairs going up from the main room and the door opening straight onto the street. They could be very bad.

It was in these houses, more than in any others, that so much depended on the woman. If she was a good home-maker, with a regular wage coming into the house, it could all be very cheerful. A bright fire burning in a well-blacked range kept the kettle singing quietly on the hob while a rag rug by the bright steel fender made a soft lie for a big purring cat. On the high mantelpiece a vase of spills on one side balanced a tea-caddy on the other from which King George V and Queen Mary, with very pink cheeks, stared out serenely. Bright-coloured cushions softened the angularities of a couple of Windsor chairs and a deal table, scrubbed to snowy whiteness, would be covered between meals with a decent cloth of crimson chenille with a fringe of bobbles round the edge. Pictures often graced the wall. 'I see you've a picture of the Holy Father,' said Thomas to one woman as the spectacled Paul in a skull-cap caught his eye, all severely, one day. 'Holy Father?' she cried, much astonished. 'Is that 'oo 'e is then? My 'usband's always told me that wor a photo of Stanley Matthews in 'is England cap!'

But misapprehensions did nothing to spoil the potential homeliness of these little houses. A bit of linoleum, spotlessly clean, would hide the stone-flagged floor, and the sweet smell of the freshly-folded ironing hanging on the pulley before the fire mingled with the aroma of the weekly baking which was cooling on a small table under the window. That was a real home. Anybody would be glad to come into a room like that at the end of the day's work, kick off his boots and draw up to the fender

148

in his stocking feet while his wife bustled about mashing the tea and getting him his bit of dinner hot out of the oven.

It was not always so. At the other end of the scale lived the poor creatures who had given up hope. Lived—or rather, dragged out their existence. Oppressed, perhaps by misfortune, by ill health, disappointment, unemployment, they had almost ceased to struggle and the circumstances of their lives were pitiful indeed. In their grates was a fire too, but a poor one, smouldering sullenly under a shovelful of slack while a big column of greenish smoke poured up the chimney and ascended sluggishly to meet the industrial pall above. On their tables was an unwiped piece of American cloth, food-stained, with a clutter of dirty dishes, sad relics of many a scanty meal; and a cloud of flies would be buzzing around the dripping, the half loaf, the sauce bottle, the open sugar packet and the half-used tin of condensed milk that remained on the table from one desolate repast to another.

The brightest spot in this stretch of the High Street was the hardware shop. Mr J., who kept it, was a jolly man. He was small and stout, and his very white hair, in a small, oiled quiff, matched his waxed moustaches which, turned up at the ends, gave his face a nice look, like a permanent smile. He wore a khaki-brown overall, a 'bratt' in Yorkshire, and he moved like a dancer on little twinkling toes round the clanging stacks of kettles and buckets and door-scrapers that crowded his shop from floor to ceiling.

He also sold paint; and when, after Nurse's and Simone's departures, we took it into our heads to paint our nursery and our rocking horse, it was he who supplied us, for ninepence, with a very old tinful. We dredged under its leathery skin and applied it, with neither much skill nor much judgement, to everything, and surprisingly, Elspeth made no objection. 'I wouldn't myself,' she explained, when I asked her about it recently, 'have *chosen* to live in a room that was sticky and blobby and coloured like melting milk chocolate—but it was your room, after all, so I said to myself "Well, if that's what they want, it's nice they can have it!" '

As well as the paint, Mr J. sold filthy pictures—or at least, they seemed filthy to me. They were postcards of the sort that you find at the sea-side, and I bought one, greatly daring, because

149

I couldn't resist it. It showed a young man, in army uniform of the first world war, with an expression of agonisingly introverted alarm running as fast as he could towards a green wooden door labelled 'W.C.' There was a short explanatory verse.

A double dose of number nine,
That's the stuff for me—
It's guaranteed to make you run—
So I'm on the double, you see!

When I had found out from Thomas about number nine ('It's a strong purgative which used to be much prescribed in the first world war—by doctors of the *regular* army, one infers . . .'), I was in a position to appreciate to the full the wit of this lyric which I thought was the subtlest I had ever heard. I put my filthy post card on my dressing table with Auntie Flo's swan pot and the crinoline lady, and it stayed there a very long time.

Further on down the street, things got brighter again, and a row of nice shops brought the village to its close with a flourish. Our grocers were down there in a perfectly lovely shop that reminded me very strongly of the emporium of Ginger and Pickles. There was the same sawdust floor, the same old-fashioned scales, the same till, the same goods, the big cheeses, the coffee beans, the sugar in sacks, the big square biscuit canisters, the butter, deftly marshalled into its pat with butter hands—everything was right. Almost nothing was pre-packed. Sugar, raisins, and tea were weighed out into little cones of paper that were flicked into shape with magical speed by experienced fingers; bacon was sliced to your taste on the great shining bacon machine, sliding to and fro in a miracle of mechanical power. Even the owners were right, with long white aprons tight round their hips just like Pickles and the same low bow as they entered the goods in the ledger and sent out the bills to everyone, 'with comp[ts].'

At the bottom of the street, down by the war memorial, was the most individual shopkeeper of them all—Rawland Keighley. It was Roland, really; but everyone pronounced it Rawland until you came to think of him as that, and never called him anything else. Rawland was the fishmonger and game merchant, and he was the sort of Yorkshireman that William the Conqueror must have hated. I am sure it was not just by chance that it was Yorkshire that William had to lay waste because its inhabitants had upped and massacred one of his garrisons. Yorkshiremen (and I say it with pride) have always been an awkward, stubborn, bloody-minded, ungovernable lot—independent is one word for it; stiff-necked is another. And so stiff was Rawland's neck that it spilled over from merely an attitude of mind to an actual physical characteristic. That tiny little jerk of the neck, usually described as 'a chuck of the head', with which northerners acknowledge one another was refined in him to the merest twitch of the muscles, a token of a movement rather than the actual thing. He looked as if his neck vertebrae might almost be fused together— it was a surprise to discover that he could still turn his head. He was a small man, but a certain forward thrust of the chin, a down-turning, trap-like mouth, a wary raised eyebrow, and a solid stance, feet well planted and knees strapped back, gave him such a look of controlled pugnacity that you instinctively treated him with circumspection. Usually his personality rather belied his appearance and he was cheerful and amiable, but there was a crusty streak which sometimes came uppermost. On one occasion during the war he sent up some turbot (it is amazing to realise that even in those days shops still delivered) which my mother sent back again, declaring that it was bad. Later in the day she called in at the shop to speak to him about it, to find him furiously indignant over the slight to his fishmongerly reputation. 'T'fish is all reet!' he shouted, thumping his fist on the marble slab, and making all the kippers jump in their boxes. 'Ah s'll send it oop to Mrs Bodger in t'mornin!' A threat which delighted my mother, because Mrs Bodger was an exceedingly tiresome, blue-rinsed, purse-proud nouveau riche, and the weather was hot, and Rawland had no refrigerator. 'Yes, do', she advised him. 'I'm sure she'll be delighted with it . . .' We often wondered whether he did.

Rawland was something of a rough diamond in his conversation, and trimmed his speech for no man—or woman. 'Ah were oop in t'market this morning,' he told my mother one day, 'But it wor no good—t'market were as flat as a fart.' A striking image which makes you wonder which kind of flatness was in his mind

—flat like a plate, or like a false note in the French horn? Another time he was talking to Thomas about an old friend of his, a shopkeeper recently retired, whom he had met by chance at the morning market. 'And ah says to 'im "How are yer gettin' on then lad, how d'you like being retired?" And he says to me "Ee Rawland" 'e says "it's grand—Ah bin kissing other folks' arses for forty year—they can kiss my booger now!" ' Whereupon he slapped his thigh under his fish-scaly navy-blue apron, and laughed until the tears ran down his cheeks.

After Rawland's shop you were at the end, and the village abruptly became country. It is one of the strangest features of the North, how the country comes up to the town. There is no belt of waste or debatable land, it is one thing or the other, and when you stand in a mill yard with the great clack and bustle of manufacture going on all round you it is curious to realise that on the other side of that seven-foot wall is a nice field, full of cows, grazing.

FIFTEEN

CHRISTMAS

All the seasons were lavish at East Gate. Spring, when the garden was crowded with rustling daffodils, and the fat crimson catkins of the elms showed knobbed against a pale, reserved blue sky. Summer, when the garden spilled over with its high tide of scented flowers, and people, passing on the street, would pause, just their heads showing above the high wall, to gaze at them and incidentally at us, as we lay on the grass in our sun-dresses and studied our Chaucers or our *Gray's Anatomy's*. Autumn, when the velvet curtains were drawn to shut out the raw drizzling dusk, and we all drew closer round the noble fire in the drawing room and Elspeth came in with a smell of the cold air about her and produced a bag of Danish pastries for tea; and above all, Christmas. Christmas, more than any other time, was the heart of the East Gate year, the round, the perfect, the golden distillation of all its qualities of warmth and hospitality. At Christmas we gathered our relations from far and near and did our best to entertain them royally, and I believe they looked forward to it as much as we did.

Christmas was Elspeth's annual triumph, and year by year I used to marvel at the remarkable efficiency with which she organised the whole thing. It was a busy time in the practice, being the natural season for colds and 'flu, but in spite of her full load of medical work she would knock off all the arrangements for a house-party of twelve to fifteen people, and a Christmas dinner for, say, twenty-two, as easily as I could write a limerick, and no detail was ever overlooked.

As Christmas approached, there was a great re-shuffling of bedrooms, a getting-out of collapsible beds, an airing of mattresses, pillows and blankets, and a counting of sheets and pillowcases. We had a big walk-in linen cupboard at East Gate, with slatted shelves, but unfortunately the air was too dirty for the linen to be kept openly stacked on them, starched and lavendered, in the Isaak Walton tradition that my romantic nature would have enjoyed. Instead, all that met your eyes when you went in there was a row of shabby brown paper parcels, mundane wrappings which protected the sheets and towels from the ever-present soot, which would otherwise have made them dirty before they had ever had an opportunity of getting as far as the beds. There was plenty of everything, though, when the parcels were undone, and I used to go from room to room, feeling rather like a chambermaid, with the fine linen sheets and matching pillow-cases over my arm, putting everything ready and turning the mattresses which sat steaming in front of the gas fires until everything was warm and dry and toasty, like the smell of an ironing blanket, when the beds could be made up ready.

But the bedrooms were of course only a minor note in the preparations, and it was the catering side that absorbed most of Elspeth's attention, and called forth her deftest manipulations of the many strands that composed her life. She would do the shopping as she went along, a bit at a time, and the mountains of provisions would accumulate in a trickle that began in the second week of December and became an avalanche as the great day drew nearer.

We had wonderful cellars at East Gate—indeed, I have never seen better ones. The whole downstairs of the house was mirrored below the ground, giving us three large square rooms, all equipped with big stone tables in the centre and two thick stone shelves round three of their walls, and a small wine cellar which was completely without any windows at all and which consequently maintained a perfect temperature for the storage of wines. All of the cellar was neatly whitewashed, and was paved with big damp flags of sandstone, and it was into this cool and capacious storage space that the results of Elspeth's shopping forays were put.

The turkey, which was enormous, would be sent up from a farm in Lincolnshire by train. It would be in the condition known as New York Dressed, which is to say plucked but not eviscerated, and would be delivered with its label round its ankle, but otherwise completely naked, by the railway people, just as if it was an ordinary parcel. It would arrive several days before Christmas and would be hung by its feet from one of the hooks in the cellar ceiling until Christmas Eve, when Thomas would take it away to the dispensary and remove its bowels with surgical precision. Then, stuffed and oven-ready, it would go back to the cellar again, but into the big meat-safe this time, as it no longer had any feet left to hang by. Jostling it in the meat-safe would be the great joints bought in ready for the other dinners of the Christmas period—a sirloin, perhaps, and a leg of pork, just to tide us over until the shops opened again . . .

Other hooks in the cellar would be crowded with other poultry in the week leading up to Christmas. There was always a goose, which we ate a couple of days after Christmas, and a couple of ducks and a chicken or two which were destined to be given away as Christmas presents. A ham, large and whole, hung by a loop of string tightly tied round its hock. Other comestibles accumulated as the week wore on until the place seemed provisioned for a seige. There were sacks of potatoes—big ones for us, and small ones for the hens; nets of sprouts and carrots; plaited strings of onions hanging against the cellar walls; a big crock of bread, with ten or fifteen large loaves in it, covered with a clean tea-towel; another crock of eggs, pickled in waterglass during the time of excessive plenty in the summer; boxes of dessert apples, Cox's orange pippins, in muted streaky green and orange, smelling richly; there were bags of nuts in all their different kinds—walnuts, brazils, almonds, hazels, even peanuts; there were flat, square cardboard boxes of tangerines individually wrapped in silver paper, adding a spicy note to the bouquet; there were bunches of grapes, delicately lemony, and indeed there were lemons themselves; there were oranges in a basket, with two or three little pineapples for Christmas Day dessert; there were flat triangular splitwod boxes of muscatel raisins and oval ones of dates; there were chocolates and Turkish delight; there was a great green puff of parsley, smelling herby; there were bunches of bananas; there were pints of cream.

Up at ground level the preparations in the kitchen gradually accelerated to keep pace with this massive underwork. Silver and china normally put away was fetched out for the occasion and great cleanings took place. We had one particular dinner service that was only used for Christmas, spending the rest of the year in tall cupboards in the room that we knew as the Long Kitchen, tucked away rather disgracefully on the other side of the back door lobby. At some time during Advent we wrestled back the dreadfully stiff sliding doors of the Long Kitchen cupboards and reverently fetched out our Christmas set for its annual period of usefulness—for which, of course, it being Yorkshire, it had to be prepared with a very thorough wash and polish.

It was a beautiful set. It was earthenware, not china, and had originally been for twenty-four people, although some of the pieces had been broken over the years. The plates were large and thick, with a crimped border. They were cream in colour, decorated with exquisite botanical prints, hand-coloured, of various flowers—a big spray across the middle of the plate and a smaller one, of something different, on the rim. There were about twenty different designs—bluebells, wild orchids, brambles, dog-roses, cabbage roses, and so on—so every piece was different. They were made by Copeland—presumably before that august firm joined forces with Spode.

Now these plates came out of hibernation every Christmas, and every Christmas they were washed up, over the course of the festivities, about a dozen times. Often enough this washing-up was done by our two very dear daily women. One of them, Mrs W., had been with us since time out of mind; the other, Mrs Er, for about six years. Her real name was Mrs Haw, but as something in Elspeth's subconscious could not quite come to terms with this as a name, I never heard her address the good lady as anything except . . . 'Mrs . . . Er . . . Er . . .' and Mrs Er was what we always called her. Now during six years it must have fallen to Mrs Er's lot to wash the Copeland dinner service up at least forty times, yet it was at the end of this lapse of time that she came to my mother one day with a very long face. 'D'you want to know summat, Mrs 'orner?' she said, lugu-briously. 'Ah were washin' that china, and I joost noticed. It isn't a set!'

As well as washing the Copeland dinner service we also washed all the best glasses, and polished the best silver, which lived in a beautiful seventeenth century set of drawers in the dining room. It was a relief to use the best knives for a while

156

because they were so beautifully blunt. All the everyday knives were victims of one of Papa's whims; when he carved the meat (which he did quite often if Thomas's surgery went on a bit late in the evening), he liked to do so with an ordinary table knife, honed to razor sharpness. He had a very high standard in this, and would go through the drawer sharpening knife after knife until he found one that came up to his expectations. The result, of course, was a drawer full of knives that would have gladdened the heart of Sweeney Todd, and reaching in briskly to get out a bundle of knives to lay the table was like putting your hand into the hole of the asp; it was unlikely to emerge in good order.

Christmas preparations on the culinary side had, of course, been going on for some time, with things like the cake and the pudding being got out of the way in October or November. It was quite a family business making these essential good things. There were raisins to be stoned, for one thing, a long and sticky job that everyone could help with, and many layers of grease-proof paper to be cut to shape for the lining of the cake tin, which was further insulated with thick waddings of brown paper round the outside before it was entrusted to the oven. The pudding was mixed in a big old-fashioned mixing-bowl, red earthenware on the outside and yellow glaze on the inside, and was stirred in ritual silence by every member of the family for a wish, before being spooned into the basin and put on for its first long steaming. I say 'it'; it was 'they' really, for our standard pudding recipe, which contained breadcrumbs, grated carrot and brandy as well as inordinate quantities of dried fruit, was enough for about five puddings of various sizes. The silver Christmas charms were all put into one particular pudding which was earmarked for the great day, and Elspeth sat up late in the steamy kitchen with puddings a-bubble on every available hot surface giving them their full five hours' worth and making sure that they didn't boil dry in the meantime.

At the top of our road was a big wholesale bakery whose delivery vans, backing and filling to get out of one another's way as they went in and out of the loading bays, performed a con-tinuous stately gavotte that you had to learn to dodge through when you wanted to catch the Bradford bus. Our Christmas cake always went up there to be professionally iced, though I never knew whether this was a service offered to the public in general or a particular favour meted out to Lady Doctor Mrs Horner by some grateful patient as a thank-you for services rendered. At any rate, they always did it for us and it would return to us transmogrified into some baroque fantasia of royal icing, but still wonderfully moist, cherry-packed and alcoholic inside. Of course we never quite knew in advance what it would look like; it was all according to the whim of the particular baker it was allotted to and sometimes it came home wild indeed. One year it reappeared as a symphony in a variety of pale greens, with a couple of adventitious Eskimo dolls on it, who looked rather as if they had accidentally wandered into a deserted public swimming-bath. But it still tasted good.

What with all the bustle and rout, the special, beautiful things brought out and got ready, the buying, hiding and wrapping of presents, and the final touches of holly and mistletoe on every ledge and picture, my excitement would be almost suffocating by the time the first guests arrived. Among the earliest arrivals would be the Ramsden cousins, who would drive up from London, and their advent always heralded the end of the preparations and the beginning of festivities, epitomised for me by moving out of my bed onto a mattress on the floor and sleeping thenceforward in something that was more like a dormitory than a bedroom.

After Christmas dinner there was always a great joke-telling among the more ribald members of the family, and anyone who had heard a good story in the course of the year saved it up for this occasion. But when the five of us cousins all got together in one bedroom, happy to be together again after months of separation, we couldn't resist giving each other a sneak preview of our carefully hoarded contributions and we used to roll about with mirth on our mattresses on the floor stuffing sheets and pillowcases into our mouths to try to stifle our giggles until we were nearly sick.

Auntie Mary was a marvellous cook, and she would usually spend the day of Christmas Eve in the kitchen knocking up a few last-minute things like mincepies and a Yule Log, and to this day I never make a mince pie without thinking of her. That particular trim on a mince pie of three little snips with the scissors, that looks like a tiny Christmas tree had its own religious meaning, she would tell me. 'Father (snip) Son (snip) and Holy Ghost (snip) you're meant to say' she would explain, suiting the action to the words faster than I can write it down; and another batch would be slid into the oven to emerge brown and glistening, ten minutes or so later, until fifty or sixty of them were piled up, spicily fragrant, on the cooling trays on the table under the window.

The last guests to arrive were Uncle George C. and Auntie Phyllis (Thomas's sister) from London who came up on the Pullman on Christmas Eve. George epitomised the blend of ability and frivolity that I so loved in my family, and in spite of being the head of a Civil Service department he could cut a caper that would have left Sir Andrew standing. ('Art thou good at these kickshawses, knight?') They always travelled first class, and one year he intrigued and puzzled his rather stuffy fellow-passengers on the Yorkshire Pullman by means of a small artificial moustache which he alternatively put on or pulled off every time he blew his nose. He was the author of a legal text book which became a standard work for all law students to study, but he often used to complain gently because he had not yet had any offers for the pantomime rights. 'I should like to see it on ice, too . . .' he would sigh, wistfully.

Christmas Day itself began early. When we were little we would find our presents in bulging pillow-cases at the end of our beds, but by the end of the war we were too old for this, and the present-giving ceremony took place after breakfast.

Breakfast itself was entirely traditional. The ham that had hung on its hook in the cellar was boiled whole in the big, black, salmon-sized fish-kettle, then stripped of its skin and coated with golden raspings, and it was ham that formed the basis of our breakfast year by year. It was so easy. The ham, with one of Papa's deadly knives, was put on the serving table in the dining room with a loaf or two, the toaster, the Cona coffee machine, and an enormous pot of stinging-fresh mustard, and everybody carved for themselves as they came down. It was immensely convenient as well as a great treat in itself and for my part I ask for no better a breakfast at any time of the year than a pink, fresh, mellow, moist home-boiled ham.

After breakfast had been eaten and cleared away, we all went into the drawing room where the presents were distributed and unwrapped, to the accompaniment of a lot of promiscuous thank-you kissing—powdery, scented kissings of aunts aimed over your shoulder for the mutual protection of lipstick, rib-cracking, hearty, fresh-shaved-cheek kisses of uncles, dimples and blushes from cousins—it was all a great whirl as one navigated on one's voyage of thankfulness through the ever-rising tide of paper among the drawing-room chairs.

A glance at the clock brought the thanking and present-showing to an end and everybody bustled upstairs with their new-found possessions while the paper was hastily swept away. For we always had a few people in to drinks on Christmas morning, and at least a semblance of decency must be restored to the room before the visitors should arrive. The vicar and his wife always came, hot from Matins, and the partners and their wives, and occasionally a patient or two, and scarcely were they all absorbed, glass in hand, into the milling throng that was our family than the moment would be upon us that more than anything else epitomised Christmas for me—the arrival of the Salvation Army.

Year after year they streamed modestly into our garden by the little green door in the high wall that was hardly ever used, ranged themselves into a big semi-circle on the sodden top lawn between the wych elm and the weeping ash, coughed, shook the spit from their instruments, and began to play in the raw, grey, misty air. It was always the same tune, 'Hail, Smiling Morn'. Somehow you never seem to hear this piece anywhere outside Yorkshire, yet in that county it is the number one choice for Christmas music, giving points and a beating to even 'Hark the Herald' and 'O come, all ye faithful'.

So every year they stood in a half-moon and played it for us while we opened the front door and went out onto the steps and we all beamed at one another; and then one of the sisters would come up with a collecting tin and Thomas and the Uncles would all stuff folded-up pound notes into it, and they would ask us for requests and play two or three more carols for us, 'Christians Awake,' perhaps, or 'While Shepherds Watched,' or 'See Amid the Winter Snow.' Then they would shake out their instruments

160

again and troop away with many cries of 'Merry Christmas', into the long, bare-treed street. Even now when I hear a Salvation Army band playing carols tears come to my eyes, which is not a thing that very often happens to me.

After our guests and the Blessed Army had departed, we began to prepare lunch and over the years a curious tradition grew up that we should have it in the consulting room. It sounds an odd venue, but virtually every other downstairs room was in some way unsuitable by now. The drawing room was dishevelled after the drinks party; the kitchen in full flood of preparation for the evening's jollities. The dining room was already in the early stages of preparation for the evening too, so that only left the surgery, and the consulting room was more inviting than the waiting-room, so thither we all repaired. Another development of tradition was that we always had salmon sandwiches for lunch on Christmas Day, followed by mince pies and tea, so we all crowded in, sitting in rows on the desk, the dressings cabinet and the examination couch while the coke fire glowed cheerily and the silver dishes passed from hand to hand.

After lunch, those who wanted to got into the car and went for a walk. This is not quite as paradoxical as it sounds; they drove for about ten minutes and walked, briskly, for about an hour, for the sake of their livers, but there was too much to do to go far. My own particular pre-occupation was with the Christmas dinner table and it was to this that I addressed myself as soon as we got back in the raw twilight of four o'clock which is evening in Yorkshire in December.

We always took a good deal of trouble with the table. To accommodate the twenty or so guests the mahogany table had to be extended to its full size and the oak gate-leg put to it at the far end. Two Irish damask table-cloths would be needed to cover this expanse, and on this virgin surface we attempted, year by year, to create a centrepiece that was both beautiful and different. One year I arranged some Christmas roses, stemless, like water lilies in a big pewter charger and added a set of eight little white china horses in oriental attitudes that my Uncle Mac had given me. A wreath of fir twigs round the edge of the charger linked it with four silvery pewter candlesticks with tall white candles in them, stretching away down the table, and a smaller wreath surrounded little red candles on circles of cardboard heaped with salt which stood in front of each place.

The most memorable of our table centres, for more reasons than one, was created by Thomas. From a half-forgotten fairy story—maybe from the Arabian Nights—he recalled a legend of an emperor who had fallen into an enchanted sleep under a tree hung with magical golden bells, so he set about making the tableau. A gnarled, twiggy branch from a little tree in the garden was scrubbed up and highlighted with subtle touches of red and gold, and planted in the middle of a low mound made of roughed-up papier mâché on a big plate. Small medicine-bottle corks, gilded, swung from its boughs in a convincing simulation of the bells, and the emperor, fashioned of clay from the garden, dreamed his enchanted sleep in a lifelike attitude beneath it, knees slightly bent and head pillowed comfortably on his hand, in a gorgeous painted robe of green and gold. It was really lovely.

It was not completely finished until the afternoon of Christmas Day when it took its place in the middle of the table and was much acclaimed, with the gilding flickering in the candlelight and the little bells trembling in the hearty bursts of laughter that shook the room. It was still looking beautiful on Boxing Day. But the day after, one began to be aware of a certain heaviness in the atmosphere of the dining room; people walking in would pause and sniff enquiringly, and when the remains of the turkey were brought in two or three suspicious glances were shot at it. On the next day it was worse and there were theories mooted about mice dying under floorboards or giblets dragged under a low piece of furniture by the cat. We got down on our knees and flashed torches under everything, but there was nothing there that could possibly be the cause of the now almost palpable odour that hung, like a corpse at a feast, about our meals until we seriously began to consider eating, for the time being, in the kitchen.

It was, of course, the emperor. Or rather not exactly the emperor, but the bank on which he was reclining, whose papier mâché middle, compounded of torn-up paper mixed with flour-and-water paste, turned out when we finally tracked it down to have degenerated into a rotting mess of deliquescence giving off this frightful miasma of decay like the ghost of Christmas Past

162

turned inside out (as Thomas's schoolmate might have said) and whitewashed.

Tea was a scratch meal on Christmas Day, with mince pies and the Christmas cake for those who wanted it, but most of us were galloping off in all directions busy with last-minute preparations and at best seized a cup and a bite on the run. There was still such a lot to do. 'Richard, could you get a good scuttle of coal for the drawing-room fire? Nice pieces!' (Elspeth always felt impelled to add this rider, though she was always teased about it.) 'Gillian, can you see that there are plenty of glasses ready for drinks before dinner? Tommy's seeing to the wines . . . Elizabeth, you're doing the place cards, aren't you?' Everybody bustled about on their allotted tasks or made last-minute preparations to their clothes. The iron was in constant use in the kitchen as sisters, mothers, aunts and cousins all jostled to give a last-minute press to their dresses, and the stairs were loud with the plaintive voice of the male sex as the uncles, brothers and fathers sought their best ties or their cuff-links or the black putting-on shoe brush which they had put down only two minutes ago *just there*.

The kitchen seethed with cooking and the Esse roared to try and keep up with the endless demand for bath-water. Even the immersion heater switched on to help it failed to stanch the depletion and by the time we young ones got a turn in the bathroom it was a choice between having somebody else's water or bathing in cold, an alternative that never gave us pause for a moment. We always opted for dirty but hot without a moment's hesitation, and one Christmas when the first comers had been particularly extravagant I had the bath eighth and Bruce, even worse, after me, was ninth!

Bruce was another kind of victim one Christmas, in a way the victim of his own good nature. He was about twelve at the time and growing immensely fast, and like many very tall young boys he had an enormous appetite. Everybody knew this and automatically gave him a vast plateful of food at every meal followed by a second helping, and normally this was just what he wanted. But on this Christmas it became too much of a good thing through an unfortunate chain of circumstances. Christmas dinner at East Gate was, as always, lavish. 'Anyone for second helpings?

163

Papa? Molly? No need to ask Bruce, let's have your plate ...
stuffing? sausages? leg or breast? Pass Bruce the bread sauce ...'
and so on. That was fine. But the next day Bruce's father, Uncle
Jim, took his children to visit his sister who lived in Bradford
and they had Christmas dinner all over again. 'More turkey,
Bruce? I know you like a lot! Look, have some more! There's
plenty! Would you like to try a glass of port afterwards?' and so
on again. Bruce smiled, accepted, ate and drank, and began to
feel that for once in his life, enough might be as good as a feast.

But the great trial was still to come. For that evening as always
on Boxing Day, our whole party went up to our dear friends the
Masons and there we had Christmas dinner yet again and still
Bruce's reputation went in front of him. 'Is that Bruce's helping?
Put a bit more on, love, he's a big lad! You like your food, don't
you, love?' Bruce, feeling bad but too shy to say so, forced it
down. No sooner had he cleared his plate than the hospitable
Masons whipped it away again and re-loaded it, brushing away
his earnestly negative noises as mere polite formalities, and then
watched him with loving gratification while he ate it. Then there
was Christmas pudding with lots and lots of cream ...

Bruce spent a wretched night being sick about eight times and
learned that it is sometimes better to be firm than to be polite.
But luckily the experience didn't entirely put him off Christmas
dinner.

In the late 40s and early 50s we had the good fortune to have
as our gardener a dear little man called Mr Wicker, who had
been a cook in the army; and for several years he came in for a
few hours on the evening of Christmas Day to do the last-minute
cooking and dishing-up, which was lovely because it meant that
all we females could get dressed and made-up in plenty of time
without having to worry about getting hot turkey fat on our
silks and satins—and, besides, he washed up afterwards. Our
dear Mrs W. and her husband usually came down and joined him
in the kitchen where they enjoyed a party of their own with lots
or beer which made Mr Wicker's face even redder than usual
and his conversation even more inconsequential. He was a great
man for multiple negatives. 'I can't see that turkey not being
done before the potatoes no how, no, not me' he would say,
leaving you wondering whether he thought it would or wouldn't.

The dinner itself was rather like a French festal meal in that it went on for two or three hours. Course succeeded course: shrimp cocktail, perhaps, with a light hock; the turkey, with all its traditional tracklements and champagne; Christmas pudding, wreathed in blue flames, with hot mince pies, fruit salad or trifle as options and Château Yquem in your glass; dessert, with great pyramids of fruit recalling the opulence of Edwardian days, with nuts, raisins and sweetmeats in little silver dishes, and decanters of port and madeira circulating in formal progression; and finally cognac, or armagnac if you preferred it, or liqueurs, of which Thomas had a prodigious selection including a revolting violet one that looked like methylated spirits and tasted of scent; and then coffee, strong and black, in the silly little demi-tasses which seemed always so inadequate, though it is true that there would not have been room by that time for a much bigger cupful of anything. It was all very traditional and foreseeable, year by year, and we loved it.

Individual moments stand out in the remembered whirl of lights, scents, laughter, pretty dresses and flowing abundance. There was the time that my mother's brothers, Archey and Percy (or 'Bill' and 'Mac'), decided to make the thin, lemony arrowroot sauce that their mother had always provided to go with the Christmas pudding. Unluckily they had no idea of the recipe and by the time they came to eat it, their arrowroot sauce had assumed the approximate texture of a squash ball, and could only be persuaded by a knife to leave its jug, when it bounced all in one lump, onto the table . . .

There was my father's cousin Molly, so beautiful and elegant, who liked a cigar, and on that one occasion each year indulged herself, and sat there looking most dashing as she drew on the large mouthpiece of a Corona Corona . . .

There was my Uncle George P., who, having gone out to the kitchen to re-fill a water jug, encountered Papa's dog Prince in the hall and, imagining himself unheard, said to him very briskly indeed 'Get out of the way, you farting bastard.' By chance this remark coincided with a momentary lull in the conversation in the dining room, and he was surprised at the storm of applause that greeted his re-entry . . .

There was the occasion when the other Uncle George, George

C., told a story so funny that it made Thomas cry, and he sat there in his chair mopping his eyes with a table-napkin and crowing for breath while the tears trickled down his red cheeks . . .

And there was always the final and most memorable delight of creeping away at the end, full up, ribs sore with laughing and dog-tired, to one's own bed where one sank into a deep blissful sleep to the sound of the owls calling in the garden and the distant shunting of the trains in the goods-yard, in the comfortable knowledge that although Christmas had come and gone again, there would be another one next year.